YOUR MYTHIC JOURNEY

Also by Sam Keen

Gabriel Marcel

Apology for Wonder

To a Dancing God

Voices and Visions

Beginnings without End

Life Maps (with Jim Fowler)

What to Do When You're Bored and Blue

The Passionate Life

Faces of the Enemy

Also by Anne Valley-Fox

Sending the Body Out

YOUR MYTHIC JOURNEY

Finding Meaning in Your Life through Writing and Storytelling

SAM KEEN

and

ANNE VALLEY-FOX

JEREMY P. TARCHER, INC.
LOS ANGELES

Library of Congress Cataloging in Publication Data

Keen, Sam.
  Your mythic journey/Sam Keen and Anne Valley-Fox.
  p. cm.
  Updated ed. of: Telling your story. 1973.
  1. Self-perception. 2. Myth--Psychological aspects. I. Fox,
Anne Valley. II. Keen, Sam. Telling your story. III. Title.
BF697.5.S43K44 1989   89-33222
155.2--dc20   CIP
ISBN 0-87477-543-4

Jeremy P. Tarcher, Inc.
5858 Wilshire Blvd., Suite 200
Los Angeles, CA 90036

Distributed by St. Martin's Press, New York

Design by Tanya Maiboroda

Manufactured in the United States of America
10 9 8 7 6 5 4

To Joseph Campbell

Cherished friend
Lover of stories
Master of myth

CONTENTS

PREFACE

by Sam Keen

A human being is a featherless,
storytelling animal.

SANDOR McNAB,
The Rebirth of Myth

Once upon a time in the childhood of the race, people
told stories, lived within a rich horizon of myth,
punctuated their lives with rites of passage, celebrated
the changing seasons with rituals, entertained themselves with tales about the antics of gods, goddesses,
foxes, and crows. But now we have come of age and
outgrown such childish superstitions. We have left
myth behind and entered the age of enlightenment.
Henceforth scientific method and reason will answer
our questions about how things are, technology will
give us the power to change what we don't like, and
economic realities will determine how we spend our
days. Long live the information revolution! Onward to
that brave new world of artificial intelligence and
computerized data banks that will tell us everything
we need to know. Everything except "Why?" and
"What is the meaning of my life?"

Don't believe a word of it!

To the contrary, this enlightenment notion—the
notion that we have outgrown myth—has collapsed
with a thud, and suddenly myth is the news of the day.
The old myths of the hero have come roaring back in
new garments in the *Star Wars* trilogy. Feminists have
revived the myths of the goddess and are busy inventing new rituals and rites of passage. Bill Moyers's
television series with Joseph Campbell, the great
mythologist who died in November 1988, received

*The psychological dan-
gers through which ear-
lier generations were
guided by the symbols
and spiritual exercises of
their mythological and
religious inheritance, we
today . . . must face
alone. . . . This is our
problem as modern, "en-
lightened" individuals,
for whom all gods and
devils have been rational-
ized out of existence.*
JOSEPH CAMPBELL,
Hero with a Thousand Faces

the kind of attention usually reserved for rock stars or quarterbacks, and Campbell's *The Power of Myth* and *Hero with a Thousand Faces* remain on the *New York Times* best-seller list week after week. It seems that Americans are finally taking seriously what Carl Jung, the Swiss psychologist, said is the most important question we can ask ourselves: "What myth are we living?"

It is possible that the failure of mythology and ritual to function effectively in our civilization may account for the high incidence among us of the malaise that has led to the characterization of our time as "The Age of Anxiety."
JOSEPH CAMPBELL,
Primitive Mythology

But why this sudden interest in mythology? If we look at the panorama of the twentieth century, it is difficult to escape the conclusion that our recent history has been shaped as much by unconscious myth as by conscious science. In the salad years of our century, Sigmund Freud warned that mythic struggles between Oedipus and the Father, Eros and Thanatos, Ego and Id are always being played out in the individual psyche beneath the fragile veneer of reason. In politics we have witnessed the demonic power of myths of race and nation—blood-dreams of an Aryan reich, a pure Yomato people, lily-white suburbs. And in God's name, various militant neo-fundamentalists in Hinduism, Judaism, Christianity, and Islam have sewn hatred and made holy wars as modern as Coke. Meanwhile, East and West have been poised on the edge of an apocalyptic battle ready to exterminate life to defend their sacred "isms." In the Vietnam era, we watched a great nation descend into tragedy because of its inability to break the spell of such mythic metaphors as *domino effect* and *containment of communism.* And everywhere that technology has carried the gospel of progress, our animal kin are dying by the species, and our watersheds are being polluted by insecticides that promised "better living through chemistry." Far from marching into a rational future, creating alabaster cities gleaming undimmed by human tears, the myth and politics of modernity have led us to a place where we are haunted by the fear that history may end either with a bang or with a whimper.

For some wild and hairy years in the 1960s, a Dionysian minority tried to throw the myths of the dominant culture to the winds. The hip and the beat dropped. out and tried to make love, not war, return power to the people, and go back to the land. With the aid of psychedelic drugs, they tripped into the underworld of the imagination and came back with tales of heroic journeys. When they needed shamans, guides, wise ones to help them understand their experience, standard-brand psychology wasn't much help. So they turned to the old myths, rediscovered Jung, the tarot, the Tibetan *Book of the Dead,* American Indian tales, Don Juan, and, of course, Joseph Campbell.

What is a myth? Few words have been subject to as much abuse and been as ill-defined as *myth.* Journalists usually use it to mean a "lie," "fabrication," "illusion," "mistake," or something similar. It is the opposite of what is supposedly a "fact," of what is "objectively" the case, and of what is "reality." In this usage myth is at best a silly story and at worst a cynical untruth. Theologians and propagandists often use myth as a way of characterizing religious beliefs and ideologies other than their own.

Such trivialization of the notion of myth reflects false certainties of dogmatic minds, an ignorance of the mythic assumptions that underlie the commonly accepted view of "reality," and a refusal to consider how much our individual and communal lives are shaped by dramatic scenarios and "historical" narratives that are replete with accounts of the struggle between good and evil empires: our godly heroes versus the demonic enemy.

In a strict sense *myth* refers to "an intricate set of interlocking stories, rituals, rites, and customs that inform and give the pivotal sense of meaning and direction to a person, family, community, or culture." A living myth, like an iceberg, is 10 percent visible and 90 percent beneath the surface of consciousness. While it involves a conscious celebration of certain values, which are always personified in a pantheon of heroes (from the wily Ulysses to the managing Lee Iacocca) and villains (from the betraying Judas to the barbarous Moammar Kadafi), it also includes the unspoken consensus, the habitual way of seeing things,

Mythology is a rendition of forms through which the formless Form of forms can be known.
JOSEPH CAMPBELL,
Primitive Mythology

It has been the chief function of much of mythological lore . . . to carry . . . the individual across the critical thresholds from . . . infancy to adulthood, and from old age to death.
JOSEPH CAMPBELL,
Primitive Mythology

the unquestioned assumptions, the automatic stance. It is differing cultural myths that make cows sacred objects for Hindus and hamburgers meals for Methodists, or turn dogs into pets for Americans and roasted delicacies for the Chinese.

The cinema, that "dream factory," employs countless mythical motifs—the fight between hero and monster, initiatory combats and ordeals, paradigmatic figures and images (the maiden, the hero, the paradisal landscape, hell, etc.).
MIRCEA ELIADE,
The Sacred and the Profane

At least 51 percent of the people in a society are not self-consciously aware of the myth that informs their existence. Cultural consensus is created by an unconscious conspiracy to consider the myth "the truth," "the way things *really* are." In other words, a majority is made up of literalists, men and women who are not critical or reflective about the guiding "truths"—myths—of their own group. To a tourist in a strange land, an anthropologist studying a tribe, or a psychologist observing a patient, the myth is obvious. But to the person who lives within the mythic horizon, it is nearly invisible.

For instance, most Americans would consider potlatch feasts, in which Northwest Indian tribes systematically destroy their wealth, to be irrational and mythic but would consider the habit of browsing in malls and buying expensive things we do not need (conspicuous consumption) to be a perfectly reasonable way to spend a Saturday afternoon. To most Americans the Moslem notion of *jihad*—holy war—is a dangerous myth. But our struggle against "atheistic communism" is a righteous duty. Ask a born-again Christian about the myth of the atonement, and you will be told it is no myth at all but a revealed truth. Ask a true believer of Marxism about the myth of the withering away of the state, and you will get a long explanation about the "scientific" laws of the dialectic of history.

Popular tales represent the heroic action as physical; the higher religions show the deed to be moral.
JOSEPH CAMPBELL,
Hero with a Thousand Faces

I suggest two analogies that may help to counteract the popular trivialized notion of myth. The dominant myth that informs a person or a culture is like the "information" contained in DNA or the program in the systems disk of a computer. Myth is the software, the cultural DNA, the unconscious information, the metaprogram that governs the way we see "reality" and the way we behave.

The organizing myth of any culture functions in

ways that may be either creative or destructive, healthful or pathological. By providing a world picture and a set of stories that explain why things are as they are, it creates consensus, sanctifies the social order, and gives the individual an authorized map of the path of life. A myth creates the plotline that organizes the diverse experiences of a person or a community into a single story.

But in the same measure that myth gives us security and identity, it also creates selective blindness, narrowness, and rigidity because it is intrinsically conservative. It encourages us to follow the faith of our fathers, to hold to the time-honored truths, to imitate the way of the heroes, to repeat the formulas and rituals in exactly the same way they were done in the good old days. As long as no radical change is necessary for survival, the status quo remains sacred, the myth and ritual are unquestioned, and the patterns of life, like the seasons of the year, repeat themselves. But when crisis comes—a natural catastrophe, a military defeat, the introduction of a new technology—the mythic mind is at a loss to deal with novelty. As Marshall McLuhan said, it tries to "walk into the future looking through a rearview mirror."

This is what fools people: a man is always a teller of tales, he lives surrounded by his stories and the stories of others, he sees everything that happens to him through them; and he tries to live his own life as if he were telling a story.
JEAN-PAUL SARTRE, *Nausea*

Every family, like a miniculture, also has an elaborate system of stories and rituals that differentiate it from other families. The Murphys, being Irish, understand full well that Uncle Paddy is a bit of a rogue and drinks a tad too much. The Cohens, being Jewish, are haunted each year at Passover when they remember the family that perished in the Holocaust. The Keens, being Calvinists, are predestined to be slightly more righteous and right than others, even when they are wrong. And within the family each member's place is defined by a series of stories. Obedient to the family script, Jane, "who always was very motherly even as a little girl," married young and had children immediately, while Pat, "who was a wild one and not cut out for marriage," sowed oat after oat before finding fertile ground.

Family myths, like those of the Kennedy clan, may

give us an impulse to strive for excellence and a sense
of pride that helps us endure hardship and tragedy. Or
they may, like the myths of alcoholic or abusive
families, pass a burden of guilt, shame, and failure from
generation to generation as abused children, in turn,
become abusive parents, ad nauseam. The sins, virtues,
and myths of the fathers are passed on to the children
of future generations.

Finally, the entire legacy and burden of cultural and
family myth comes to rest on the individual. Each
person is a repository of stories. To the degree that any
one of us reaches toward autonomy, we must begin a
process of sorting through the trash and treasures we
have been given, keeping some and rejecting others.
We gain the full dignity and power of our persons
only when we create a narrative account of our lives,
dramatize our existence, and forge a coherent personal
myth that combines elements of our cultural myth and
family myth with unique stories that come from our
experience. As my friend David Steere once pointed
out to me, the common root of "authority" and
"authorship" tells us a great deal about power. Who-
ever authors your story authorizes your actions. We
gain personal authority and power in the measure that
we question the myth that is upheld by "the authori-
ties" and discover and create a personal myth that
illuminates and informs us.

What Santayana said about cultures is equally true
for individuals: "Those who do not remember history
are condemned to repeat it." If we do not make the
effort to become conscious of our personal myths
gradually, we become dominated by what psychologists have variously called repetition compulsion,
autonomous complexes, engrams, routines, scripts,
games. One fruitful way to think of neurosis is to
consider it a tape loop, an oft-told story that we repeat
in our inner dialogues with ourselves and with others.
"Well, I'm just not the kind of person who can . . ."
"I never could . . ." "I wouldn't think of . . ." While
personal myths give us a sense of identity, continuity,
and security, they become constricting and boring

*It has always been the
prime function of my-
thology and rite to sup-
ply the symbols that car-
ry the human spirit
forward, in counterac-
tion to those other con-
stant human fantasies
that tend to tie it back.*
JOSEPH CAMPBELL,
Primitive Mythology

*Myth is the secret open-
ing through which the
inexhaustible energies of
the cosmos pour into hu-
man cultural manifesta-
tion.*
JOSEPH CAMPBELL,
Hero with a Thousand Faces

if they are not revised from time to time. To remain vibrant throughout a lifetime we must always be inventing ourselves, weaving new themes into our life-narratives, remembering our past, re-visioning our future, reauthorizing the myth by which we live.

A PERSONAL NOTE ON PERSONAL MYTHOLOGY

To the best of my knowledge, the idea of personal mythology was born on November 4, 1964, the day the ground on which I stood trembled, the day the giant fell and left me with a shattered world—the day my father died.

My father's death pulled the linchpin that held my belief system together. When my "Christian" world-view and moral horizons collapsed, I had to find a new myth by which to live. For a while I remained in terrible confusion and anxiety. Then one day it occurred to me that every people, every tribe had a mythology that gave them answers to its agonizing questions about the meaning of life. I began to study anthropology and mythology, not in an abstract, scholarly way, but to find what the stories of other peoples could tell me about my own life. I went to collections of the myths of various tribes and peoples, such as Frank Waters's *Book of the Hopi,* and analyzed the repertoire of fundamental questions and answers that were included in any mythology:

I asked myself, "What is the myth you are living?" and found that I did not know. So . . . I took it upon myself to get to know "my" myth, and I regarded this as the task of tasks . . . I simply had to know what unconscious or preconscious myth was forming me.
C. G. JUNG,
The Portable Jung

Where did I come from?
Why is there something rather than nothing?
Why is there evil in the world?
What happens to me when I die?
With whom do I belong?
How close should I be to my mother, father, brother, sister, wife, husband, cousin, son, daughter, lover, or friend?
What are my duties, my obligations?
What is taboo, and what should I avoid?

What is the purpose of my life, my vision?
Whom should I imitate?
Who are the heroes and heroines?
Who are the villains?
Who is our enemy?
What are the stages along life's way?
Who are my helpers, guides, allies?
What is disease?
How can I be purified, healed?
What should we do with bounty, wealth, surplus?
What is our relationship with animals?

The next step in creating both the notion and the technique for recovering a personal mythology came in a flash when I realized that when I asked these questions to myself, I also had a repertoire of stories within my autobiography that gave me satisfying personal answers about the meaning of my life.

Don't be satisfied with stories, how things have gone with others. Unfold your own myth.
RUMI

In telling about my discovery of the myth that was central to my life, I can do no better than to share what I wrote at the time in *To a Dancing God:*

Once upon a time when there were still Indians, Gypsies, bears, and bad men in the woods of Tennessee where I played, and, more important still, there was no death, a promise was made to me. One endless summer afternoon my father sat in the eternal shade of a peach tree, carving on a seed he had picked up. With increasing excitement and covetousness I watched while, using a skill common to all omnipotent creators, he fashioned a small monkey out of the seed. All of my vagrant wishes and desires disciplined themselves and came to focus on that peach-seed monkey. If only I could have it, I would possess a treasure which could not be matched in the whole cosmopolitan town of Maryville! What status, what identity I would achieve by owning such a curio! Finally, I marshaled my nerve and asked if I might have the monkey when it was finished (on the sixth day of creation). My father replied, "This one is for your mother, but I will carve you one someday."

Days passed, and then weeks and, finally, years, and the someday on which I was to receive the monkey did not arrive. In truth, I forgot all about the peach-seed monkey. Life in the ambience of my father was exciting, secure, and colorful. He did all of those things for his children a father can do, not the least of which was merely delighting in their existence. One of the lasting tokens I retained of the measure of his dignity and courage was the manner in which, with emphysema sapping his energy and eroding his future, he continued to wonder, to struggle, and to grow.

In the pure air and dry heat of an Arizona afternoon on the summer before the death of God, my father and I sat under a juniper tree. I listened as he wrestled with the task of taking the measure of his success and failure in life. There came a moment of silence that cried out for testimony. Suddenly I remembered the peach-seed monkey, and I heard the right words coming from myself to fill the silence: "In all that is important, you have never failed me. With one exception, you kept the promises you made to me—you never carved me that peach-seed monkey."

Not long after this conversation I received a small package in the mail. In it was a peach-seed monkey and a note which said, "Here is the monkey I promised you. You will notice that I broke one leg and had to repair it with glue. I am sorry I didn't have time to carve a perfect one."

Two weeks later my father died. He died only at the end of his life.

For me, a peach-seed monkey has become a symbol of all the promises which were made to me and the energy and care which nourished and created me as a human being. And, even more fundamentally, it is a symbol of that which is the foundation of all human personality and dignity. Each of us is redeemed from shallow and hostile life only by the sacrificial love and civility which we have gratuitously received . . . When I discover the promises made and kept which are the hidden root of my sense of the basic trustworthiness of the world and my consequent freedom to commit myself to action, I discover my links with the past; I find the "once upon a time" which is the beginning of the story I must tell to be myself.

Life has confided so many stories to me, I shall have to retell them to people who cannot read the book of life itself.
ETTY HILLESUM,
An Interrupted Life

After experimenting with my own stories, I began in 1969 to conduct seminars around the United States and Europe on "Personal Mythology." In giving these seminars, I developed the methods of self-exploration and storytelling that now make up the Viewpoints in this book. The magic of the seminars was due to the simple discovery that everyone has a fascinating story to tell, an autobiographical myth. And when we tell our stories to one another, we, at one and the same time, find the meaning of our lives and are healed from our isolation and loneliness. Strange as it may seem, self-knowledge begins with self-revelation. We don't know who we are until we hear ourselves speaking the drama of our lives to someone we trust to listen with an open mind and heart.

In 1971 I interviewed Joseph Campbell for *Psychology Today.* During the interview the Esalen Institute called and asked Joseph if he would do a seminar. He asked me, "Why don't you do the seminar with me?"

I did. And thereafter we did seminars together combining the methods of recovering personal mythology with reflection on classical mythical themes until the year before he died. My debt to him will be obvious on these pages.

Now it is time to begin your own mythic journey. Choose a confidant, a listener, an audience for your tales. You don't have to wait until you are so mad, bad, sad, and hazardous to yourself and others that you have to hire a professional listener—a therapist. Ask your husband, your wife, your child, your lover, your best friend to share this quest.

I can't promise that your stories will give you certainty or objective truth any more than the ancient myths gave the Hebrews or Greeks accurate maps of the world. They will, however, fill you with the stuff from which romance, tragedy, and comedy are made, which alone can give you an entertaining and meaningful life. They will hollow you out so you can listen to the stories of others, as common and unique as your own. And that remains the best way we storytelling animals have found to overcome our loneliness, develop compassion, and create community.

Finally, before the end of this beginning, before she introduces herself, I want to say a very few words about the coauthor of this book. Midway through life's journey my path swerved and passed through some marvelous and troubled lands—divorce, beginning again, and all that. I've written about it in *Beginnings without End* and *The Passionate Life,* if you are interested. For now, suffice it to say that for a couple of years Anne Valley-Fox (whose last name was borrowed from a fleet horse that won the sixth race at Del Mar) and I shared love stories in a kingdom by the sea. During that time we collected other people's stories, worked together daily, and gave birth to a book that was then called *Telling Your Story.* (We wanted to call it "Like the Time I Filled a Bag with Apples and Jumped on a Horse and Rode Off Forever," but the publisher said no.) In due time we took different paths, married other people, had families, authored our separate stories. But through the years our friendship has ripened, and the work we did together is as fresh as it was then. I hope you will be as enriched by the reading of this book as we were by the writing and rewriting of it.

PREFACE

by Anne Valley-Fox

When Sam took me to meet Joseph Campbell in 1972, we sat in his study—a room made of books, not walls—and he spoke with us of the danger and bliss of the hero's journey. I was twenty-five at the time, still reveling in the aftershocks of the 1960s in America— socially disillusioned, yet expecting somehow to stun the world through my personal brilliance. So I asked Campbell how it was that the hero was so often cast in masculine form. Surely women are heroic, too? He didn't respond by narrating, as I had hoped, any of the hundreds of myths at his fingertips featuring intrepid females. What he did say caused everything else we spoke of that day to fall out of my memory. He said that he and his wife, Jean, had chosen not to have children because their life's work was already cut out for them. But most women are set inexorably on the heroic path through childbirth and the challenge of maternity.

In those years I refused to think of myself in a class with "most women." I was still young and blithe enough to believe that I might transcend the human condition, which seemed to me grounded, if not buried, in marriage and the family. So sidestepping these pitfalls, I knocked about, wrote poems, and conspired with Sam to give birth to this book.

Writing and listening to stories, as I did then, I presumed that a life could be fashioned, brought under control even, through the things one said and the stories one told—just look how the storyteller's face lights up and is transformed, over and over, in the act of telling!

What I didn't realize then was how powerfully our

personal mythologies are rooted in the consciousness of all peoples in all places in all times. If I wanted to tell stories about myself in which I was a romantic gypsy, fine; there was bound to be some personal truth in that. Yet the stories I told would not finally shape my life—instead it would be the other way around. I exchanged hundreds of stories with people before I understood that one's life comes and gets one sooner or later, and all of one's gypsy stories, for instance, at last wash off and run to the great sea of wanderer mythology.

Today, nearly twenty years after this book was first written, I feel I am washed of my gypsy, my poet, my fury which set me apart, and I am, as Joseph Campbell prescribed it, a woman among women, surrounded by mate, children, friends, and world peoples journeying together some distance down a road.

Once I told stories as a person tries on suit after suit of clothes to find the most flattering fit. Now I am in my walking shoes, gladly moved, step by step, by the stories we tell and have always told.

1

To Tell a
Story

We are storytelling animals. As our primitive ances-
tors sat around the fire carving spearheads and eating
blackberries they told stories which in time were
woven into a tapestry of myth and legend. These tales
were the first encyclopedia of human knowledge.
They explained where the world came from, why
there were people, why snakes have no legs, why corn
smut stops birth hemorrhages, why conch shells are
sacred, why coyotes howl at night, and why the gods
put fire and death on earth. In the dramatic telling the
triumphs of heroes and the antics of fools came alive
again. Stories told the people of a tribe who they were,
where they had been, where they were going, and how
to stay friendly with the spirits.

Our modern myths are often unfocused; we don't
celebrate our myths enough, they frequently hide like
outlaws in the backwoods of the unconscious. For a
variety of historical reasons (the emergence of machines, cities, anonymity, money, mass media, stan-
dardization, automation) we've lost awareness of
storytelling as a way to dramatize and order human
existence. But whether we acknowledge them or not
our myths and stories live in our imaginations.

To be a person is to have a story to tell. We become
grounded in the present when we color in the outlines
of the past and the future. Mythology can add perspective and encouragement to your life. Within each of us
there is a tribe with a complete cycle of legends and
dances, songs to be sung. We were all born into rich

*All sorrows can be borne
if you put them into a
story or tell a story
about them.*
ISAK DINESEN

mythical lives: we need only claim the stories that are our birthright.

With a little imagination each person can find within himself a replacement for the myths and stories lost when we ceased living in tribes. A person is a complex being made up of a million individual smells, tastes, memories, and hopes. Listen for a few minutes to the voices that run through your mind. Every psyche is a private theater filled with scenes and characters. Listen and you will hear your father, mother, brothers, sisters, children, lovers, friends, enemies, teachers, and heroes acting out their dramas on your stage. Hearing the multiple voices within yourself will remind you that you belong to a special clan. Your people still inhabit you. They will help you to celebrate your myths, sing your songs, and tell your legends.

The techniques of storytelling and the psychology which underlies them rest on a discovery of the obvious: that what all persons have in common is their uniqueness. Every person has a story to tell. That's what makes a person and defines the journey that person makes through life. There are no autonomous, anonymous, pragmatic individuals—we were all raised by an intimate group that had traditions, values, rites of passage, ceremonies, and legends. When we forget our stories, leave our heroes unsung, and ignore the rites that mark our passage from one stage of life into another, we feel nameless and empty.

We can rediscover the uniqueness of the person if we reassemble our myths and stories which have been homogenized into business, education, politics and dissipated in the media. Find the unconscious and make it conscious, find an audience for the untold tales, and you will discover you are already on a rich mythic journey. What most of us lack is only the permission to tell the stories that are our own birthright.

You can't tell who you are unless someone is listening. There are better and easier ways to get an audience than by hiring a psychiatrist. Find a partner to

Whenever men have looked for something solid on which to found their lives, they have chosen not the facts in which the world abounds, but the myths of an immemorial imagination.
JOSEPH CAMPBELL,
Primitive Mythology

listen and tell your multiple stories, stories of your childhood, your family, your roots. Be all those characters who wander around in your head. Journey back into the past, ahead into your future, and out into cosmic time. Discover a few of your many selves.

The emphasis on telling stories amounts to a new way of defining personality and psychology. Psychology ought to be much more concerned with boredom and excitement and less concerned with mental illness and lost and found identity. The dis-ease of the modern psyche is more of a vacuum than a thorn in the flesh. If we are alienated, disgraced, frustrated, and bored, it is because of what *hasn't* happened, because of potentialities we have not explored. Few of us know the fantastic characters, emotions, perceptions, and demons that inhabit the theaters that are our minds. We are encouraged to tell a single (true) story, construct a consistent character, fix an identity. We are thus defined more by neglected possibilities than by realized ones. We rehearse and repeat a monotonous monologue while heroes and villains, saints and madmen, ascetics and libertines wait in the wings for a chance to seize center stage and run wild. In this sense, identity is a repetition compulsion, a conspiracy to put a consistent face before the world, to cover up the glorious inconsistency of emotions and desires. The character we develop domesticates the world and leaves us no wilderness to play in. There are many territories of imagination and many strange regions of emotion that we may not enter without throwing our sanity into question: Until we cross some borders, we are likely to remain rational, banal, boring, bored. A major concern of any therapeutic psychology should be to help an individual lose identity.

A psychological proposal is always political and this one proposes an ideal relationship between the individual and the community. Paradoxically, an individual becomes strongest, most vivid, and most open when he discovers the contradictions of his psyche. Each of us harbors the entire range of human possibilities. Every I is a we. We can become authentically public

Every person, then, is many persons; a multitude made into one person; a corporate body; incorporated, a corporation . . . The unity of the person is as real, or unreal, as the unity of the corporation.
N. O. BROWN,
Love's Body

We have not even to risk the adventure alone; for the heroes of all time have gone before us; the labyrinth is thoroughly known; we have only to follow the thread of the hero-path. And where we had thought to find an abomination, we shall find a god; . . . where we had thought to travel outward, we shall come to the center of our own existence; where we had thought to be alone, we shall be with all the world.
JOSEPH CAMPBELL,
Hero with a Thousand Faces

only by first going to the depths of the private. At the heart of the uniqueness of the individual lies the universal. Every person's deepest ecstasies and fears are old as mankind and common as dirt. Thus, the greatest freedom for the individual comes from the love of many stories. The strongest state is the one that keeps the fewest citizens in jails, insane asylums, and ghettos.

This book is designed to help you open the doors behind which you imprison the citizens of your private commonwealth. It is an invitation to form a community of teller and listener. It is a call to revolution; seize the authority to create your story.

2

THE KEY

Use this book as a travel guide. It provides theoretical maps (Philosophy), travel hints (Viewpoints), first-hand accounts (Stories), and references to traditional myths (Marginalia) to help you explore your own time, space, roots, and personal mythology.

The Philosophy that begins each section works as a large-scale map, a territorial overview. The broad theories of time and personality in these sections are pathways into experience. The maps chart known landmarks but leave many psychic frontiers uncharted.

The Viewpoints are designed to lead you on side trips to specific places within your mind and experience. They are like turnouts on a winding mountain road that let you see where you came from and where you are going.

The Stories are slides, souvenirs from personal journeys. We shaped and edited tales told to us by friends and by strangers on bus benches, as illustrations of the power of telling your own story.

The Marginalia provide a kind of antiphonal chorus to the text. All have been added since the initial publication of this book, and they are designed to reflect something of the process of the workshops on Personal Mythology that I [Sam Keen] conducted over the years with Joseph Campbell. In these workshops I led participants through an exploration of their personal myths, making use of the exercises and questions contained in Viewpoints. Then Joseph took over and showed the parallels between an individual's autobiographical myth and the great classical myths. And what a feast it was for all because Joseph was a living encyclopedia of myth.

Perhaps a stable order can only be established on earth if man always remains acutely conscious that his condition is that of a traveler. . . . It is precisely the soul that is the traveler; it is of the soul and of the soul alone that we can say with supreme truth that "being" necessarily means "being on the way" (en route).
Gabriel Marcel,
Homo Viator

The hero is the man or woman who has been able to battle past his personal and local historical limitations to the generally valid, normally human forms. . . .
The hero has died as a modern man; but as eternal man—universal man—he has been reborn.
JOSEPH CAMPBELL,
Hero with a Thousand Faces

These marginal references, many of them taken from Joseph's books, will provide the resonance between universal mythic themes and your own personal myth. You will find that as you explore the story of your life, you will become the companion of those heroes and heroines, philosophers and mystics who have undertaken the pilgrimage to find the secret meaning that lies hidden in the depths of every life.

It's your trip. Begin anywhere you want to—in the present, the past, the future, or in cosmic time. Do pass go! Move at your own speed. Get the lay of the land quickly, linger wherever you like the view. Mark spots of interest or mystery for later explorations. Enjoy moving or holding still.

The story is you.

3

THE PRESENT

*It's a Long Way to
Here and Now*

Intense pleasure sweeps time out of mind. In rare moments—when the sun sinks into the sea, when thoughts couple to form a metaphor, when lovers come together—all awareness focuses on the here and now. When we are absorbed in thought or action, consciousness advances gracefully along the retreating edge of the present moment and we feel spontaneous and integrated.

Most people visit the state of pure awareness and ecstasy from time to time but few can live there for long. Total concentration is as rare as it is precious. Our attention usually is split. We take mind trips into the past or the future or retreat into fog. Or we jump out of our bodies and watch ourselves with others' eyes. And watch ourselves being watched.

In modern America the rush toward the here and now has spawned a host of philosophical and psychological schools and disciplines. In the 1960s psychedelics promised to open "the door of perception" (Huxley) which lead to the Eternal Now. Gestalt therapy works to clear away past and future fantasies that inhibit full involvement in the present moment. Transactional Analysis encourages the substitution of intimacy for game playing. Zen quiets the mind and teaches the art of eating, sleeping, and walking. Group therapy and sensory awareness training aims at immediate expression of feelings and sensations.

One realm we have never conquered—the pure present. One great mystery of time is terra incognita to us—the instant. The most superb mystery we have hardly recognized—the immediate, instant self.
D. H. LAWRENCE

*My miracle is that when
I feel hungry I eat, and
when I feel thirsty I
drink.*
BANKEI, Zen master

In spite of the rhetoric of pure awareness and spontaneity most of these movements understand that there is more to being in the present moment than letting go and flowing down the river. Awareness is only as profound as the person who is aware. We learn to see and feel profoundly as we integrate all that we have been and hope to be into the present moment. The most dynamic personalities are fully present in this moment without severing either memories of the past or visions of the future.

Boredom is imprisonment in one time and place. There are four human time zones in which we can travel. We can respond to the present, remember the past, anticipate the future, or stand in wonder in the eternity of cosmic time. Cultivate the ability to be in any of these zones and the here and now will be enriched with imports from other times and places. Travelers in time and space discover stories enough for a lifetime of entertainment.

THE PUBLIC SELF

*Star Wars has a valid
mythological perspective.
It shows the state as a
machine and asks, "Is
the machine going to
crush humanity or serve
humanity?" . . . When
Luke Skywalker un-
masks his father, he is
taking off the machine
role that the father has
played. The father was
the uniform. That is
power, the state role.*
JOSEPH CAMPBELL,
The Power of Myth

Every person is composed of at least three nations— one public, one private, and one unknown. Each nation has its own boundaries, customs, laws, language, and traditions. Some boundaries are guarded and may be crossed only by trusted friends. The frontier between the known and the unknown self is always heavily guarded. No one of us can travel freely in the hidden places of his consciousness but, fortunately, messengers slip past the border guards and bring us dreams and images from the unknown. Ideally the highways that connect the nations should be well marked so that we can travel anywhere. But ignorance or fear keeps us from exploring the outer limits of ourselves.

Let's begin with the public self, the psychic territory that is supposed to be open to all—officials, acquaintances, colleagues, and strangers. The human animal is always social; there is no solitary self, no man is an island. Even when we retreat to solitude we carry within us myriad voices. When there's no one else to talk to we talk to ourselves.

The public self performs for an audience, real or fancied. It is the creation of the eyes that watch it. We learn to put on masks and costumes and play the roles society expects of us. A girl begins to learn what is expected of a woman the day her mother gives her a doll instead of an erector set. Bankers shine their wing-tips, railroad engineers climb into overalls, sailors and bikers have themselves tattooed, punk rockers shave their heads or dye their hair neon colors. By compounded example we learn the language and dress that are appropriate to our class and profession. But by changing your metaphors and images of yourself and your language, you can enlarge your public self and the possibilities open to you.

Most of us hate to admit that we conform to the dictates of groupthink. But clearly the need for social approval is as fundamental to the human animal as the need for food. Community is not a luxury for human beings. The self is created by its multiple presentations; without an audience there's no individual. So long as we do not identify totally with any single role—doctor, lawyer, merchant, chief, healer—we remain free to explore the many possibilities of the private self as well as of the public self.

No man is an Iland, intire of it selfe; every man is a peece of the Continent, a part of the maine; if a Clod be washed away by the Sea, Europe is the lesse, as well as if a Promontorie were, as well as if a Manor of thy friends or of thine own were; any man's death diminishes me, because I am involved in Mankinde.
JOHN DONNE,
"No Man Is an Iland"

Viewpoints

One way to identify your public self is to locate the words you most often use to describe yourself to others. The story of your official public self is told by the way you fill in blanks on insurance or tax forms. (name, age, sex, birthplace, marital status, police record, health, organizational affiliations). A more complex story is told by the terms you use to describe yourself to others.

All the world's a stage
And all men and
women merely players.
They have their exits
and their entrances;
And one man in his
time plays many parts.
WILLIAM SHAKESPEARE,
As You Like It

- Make a list of the ten words or phrases that describe you best. I am _____. They might be functions, feelings, activities, affiliations (ticket taker, frightened, Rotary Club president, student, competent, clown).
- Stop. If you want to do the above, do it before reading further. Many of the Viewpoints introduce perspectives from which you can spy on yourself. The element of surprise may startle you into unfamiliar positions from which you can see what you've hidden from yourself.
- Now rank the words or phrases in order of importance.
- Now cross them out (give them up) one at a time until you are left with your single most important characteristic. By relinquishing your self-definitions one at a time you will get an idea of the most prized and the least crucial levels of your public self. (With two or more playing, this can be a revealing game.)

You are both like and unlike other persons. Only you can write your autobiography. But when it is written it will be a human story. If pride depends upon the sense of uniqueness then humility rests upon awareness of our membership in humanity.

A man has many skins
in himself, covering the
depths of his heart. Man
knows so many things;
he does not know him-
self. Why, thirty or for-
ty skins or hides, just
like an ox's or a bear's,
so thick and hard, cover
the soul. Go into your
own ground and learn to
know yourself there.
MEISTER ECKHART

- In what ways are you unique? What qualities distinguish you from your friends, your enemies, the masses? Do you think other people consider you unusual? Odd? Average? A character? An individual? Unobtrusive? Hostile? Do you agree with them?
- If you were placed suddenly in an alien culture how would you identify with and distinguish yourself from the natives?
- If you were to die tomorrow how much of the story of your life could be reconstructed from what other people know of you? Who knows you best? How much of your essential self is public and how much is private? How would you be remembered?

Somebody Meets Everyman

Unique? You bet I am! Haven't I spent most of my life proving it? Look around me, the stamp of my presence is everywhere. When I was eleven I learned about birds and gave my first lecture on ornithology to the local women's sewing circle: they thought I was wonderful, no other kid in town could do that! Another high moment was when I nearly flunked out of school while I was busy becoming the youngest Eagle Scout in the history of Maryland. All along, no matter what the crowd did I did the opposite. If they wore tuxedos I would show up in Levis. I made myself intriguing by being controversial and inaccessible. I sharpened my mind against the hardest ideas and largest men around. I climbed to the top of my profession so that I knew all the best people in my field in the country, and they knew me.

But then, by God, I found out it was lonely on that mountain top. All my will power scared people off; sure I was admired, but who enjoyed me? When my father died I realized that no uniqueness in the world could save me from ending up just like everyone else. The other day I saw an idiot in a coffeehouse laughing and moaning hysterically, on and on, completely out of control, and I thought, *what a curiosity he is,* and turned away from him. But underneath I knew that the only difference between him and me was that I keep my sense of absurdity under tight control and he lets his right out—he doesn't bother to pretend.

These days I do a lot more laughing and crying, and it's a great relief. I feel more of everything. My body gives me away: it hurts, it feels good, it demands to be fed, it needs to be touched. In the end it's the common things that actually make the difference.

> —SAM, a writer and philosopher, is a Southern Calvinist transplanted to Southern California

I am not I.
I am this one
walking beside me whom
* I do not see,*
whom at times I manage
* to visit,*
and whom at other
* times I forget;*
who remains calm and
* silent while I talk,*
and forgives, gently,
* when I hate,*
who walks where I am
* not,*
who will remain
* standing when I die.*
JUAN RAMÓN JIMÉNEZ
(translated from the Spanish by Robert Bly)

The mythogenetic zone today is the individual in contact with his own interior life, communicating through his art with those "out there."
JOSEPH CAMPBELL,
Creative Mythology

THE PRIVATE SELF

The boundary between public and private is hard to distinguish. Privacy is always a matter of degree. At times we allow friends, lovers, family, or a stranger on an airplane to come behind the façade of our public images, but we often remain on stage even in intimate situations. Breadwinning husbands and housekeeping wives, for instance, can easily slip into allowing traditional sexual roles to inhibit their real desires, so that their public selves operate in the private sphere too. In this situation the deepest dimensions of privacy are experienced in isolation: the private self may be a locked inner room labeled NO ADMISSION.

Secrets come in all sizes and shapes, from adultery to xenophobia, but they cluster around the emotional centers of shame and elation. Many of the things we feel, desire, or do seem too shameful to be shared. We hide from public view fear, guilt, despair, impotence, cruelty, self-hatred, ugliness, and coldness of heart. We are afraid to let anyone see our degrading self-images, but we also conceal our tender ideals, grandiose visions, and ecstasies.

All that psychology has accomplished is to make the inner life the subject matter of science, and in doing this it dissipated the idea of the soul. But it was the soul which once linked man's inner life to a transcendent scheme of cosmic heroism.
ERNEST BECKER,
Escape from Evil

Viewpoints

Sometimes you can dispel shame or expand pleasure by sharing your secrets.

- What are the secrets that you never (or rarely) share with anyone?
- What secrets would you be relieved to share? With whom? What will become of them, once told?
- Which are easier to share—the secrets of your idealized self or those of your degraded self?

Degraded self-images revolve around feelings of fear, weakness, anger, and confusion.

- In fantasy, allow yourself to be as weak, inadequate, passive, and ineffectual as you have ever feared yourself to be. Remember the times when you have felt small and helpless.

- Imagine that you are uncontrollably angry. Describe the persons you would punish, torture, or kill, the things you would destroy.
- If you lost your reason, your inhibiting forces, what form would your madness take?

Idealized images of the self usually cluster around fantasies of love, power, perfection, beauty, fame, knowledge, or creativity.

- Create a fantasy in which you become the fulfillment of your ideal self. You are strong, loving, beautiful, brilliant, etc. What do you do with your power? What gives you the most pleasure?
- Chart the way you bounce back and forth between idealized and degraded images and feelings about yourself, between Infant and Superman, Earth Mother and Temptress, Master Builder and Caspar Milquetoast.

My Heart Was Clear as the Summer Sky

My life is full of secrets, all because I've done so many things and always had so much trouble with men. I'm outspoken by nature, but around the trailer court I try to keep my mouth shut about most things, because the older folks get offended by what I say. They don't much care for the plain truth.

My heart was clear as the summer sky until I lost Mick. We were married at eighteen and stayed passionately in love for eight years. Can you believe it? Then one night I was playing pinochle like I always did when Mick was working late, and I had the feeling that there was a ghost in the room. I kept looking up and around and swishing the air with my hand and then later they came in and told me he'd just been electrocuted in the mine, my Mick was dead. It must have happened fast because there was a great big grin on his face, but it wasn't so easy for me. All my hair fell out from grief.

I have a habit of falling in love. But ever since I lost Mick I fall *out* fast too—one good cry will do it. I've had a lot of experiences that I don't talk about much, mostly because

It is easier to sail many thousands of miles through cold and storm and cannibals, in a government ship, with five hundred men and boys to assist one, than it is to explore the private sea, the Atlantic and Pacific Ocean of one's being alone.
HENRY DAVID THOREAU, *Walden*

The secret thoughts of a man run over all things, holy, profane, clean, obscene, grave and light, without shame or blame.
THOMAS HOBBES

people don't believe them, they get uncomfortable and shut right up. My longest secret is probably about Charlie. He was my boss when I was widowed in Oregon, and after a long time I got pregnant by him. He loved me but he couldn't marry me because he already had a family, so I real quick married someone else. Once when my son was five or six I ran into Charlie in a restaurant in Seattle. He got very drunk and told my son that he had three daughters and a half son whose mother he would always love in his heart. When my son was eighteen I told him that his father was someone long gone, but nobody else ever knew. Even my husband thought that he fathered that kid.

After a dozen stormy years with my second husband we split up and I moved north. I opened a restaurant on the Canadian border which really brought in the money, but then I got hooked up with Harold, a good-looking fellow with the charm of a rattlesnake, and that man tricked me out of half a million dollars! Harold chased pretty girls and misused me, so finally I let him go. After that divorce I decided that what I really needed was to get me a man who carried a lunch pail.

This be my pilgrimage and goal
Daily to march and find
The secret phrases of the soul
The evangels of the mind.
JOHN DRINKWATER

So I found Oley and stopped running around with the wealthy set and moved out of my beautiful house on the hill to come here and live quietly. Oley's just about the sweetest person I ever met except that he's got this drinking problem and doesn't admit it so I have to cover up for him all the time. Oley's problem makes one more secret in my life, that and the fact that he and I aren't married the way we say we are. Making it legal again just doesn't seem like a good idea. We've been together for a few years and maybe it'll last, but you can never be sure.

The thing I secretly wish is that Mick and I could have stuck together all the way through, but death doesn't make allowances for happiness. You go from lover to lover and place to place and after a while you start getting confused. Things don't stick together the way they used to, it's hard to tell what's what. And in the end there's nobody that really knows you.

—LUCILLE is a Midwesterner in her fifties
who lives with her cats in a trailer court

The Unknown Self

Consciousness is like a lantern on a dark night illuminating everything within a circle. When it's carried from one place to another some new obscurity surrounds the circle of clarity. What we know about ourselves is in continual dialogue with darkness. Self-knowledge and ignorance are linked because of the selective structure of the human mind. In focusing attention on one thing we ignore another.

The unknown self contains all of those experiences, feelings, fantasies, and possibilities that we repress rather than act out. This unconscious life erupts in dreams, slips of the tongue, projections of anger and love. What we don't know *does* hurt us and help us.

Happiness is free flow between your known and unknown selves, trust in the compatibility of conscious and unconscious. The more we venture into the psychic depths the more likely we are to discover that the unknown is not peopled with enemies.

Viewpoints

The known and the unknown are in constant dialogue. Look at one and you will get a reflection of the other.

- In an earlier Viewpoint you listed ten words and phrases that characterized you. Now make a list of ten characteristics you do *not* have—qualities, functions, feelings, or roles you find it important to deny. What characterizations would you strongly deny if they were applied to you (dumb, manipulative, weakling, homosexual, gentle, introverted)?
- Stop. If you want to catch your unknown self off guard, do the above before reading further.

One of Freud's basic rules for understanding the unconscious is that a negation is as good as an affirmation. What you strive to deny defines you as much as

The shadow is a moral problem that challenges the whole ego-personality, for no one can become conscious of the shadow without considerable moral effort. To become conscious of it involves recognizing the dark aspects of the personality as present and real. This act is the essential condition for any kind of self-knowledge, and it therefore, as a rule, meets with considerable resistance.
C. G. Jung,
The Portable Jung

what you affirm. One way to explore the unknown self is to turn everything upside down. Assume that you are what you aren't and that you aren't what you are. Flip your story.

- Take your list of negations and compose convincing arguments to prove that these are your most essential qualities.
- Now take your earlier list of ten affirmations and show that these qualities do *not* characterize you. The most important and the least important qualities are to be reversed.

Nothing determines who we will become so much as those things we choose to ignore.
SANDOR McNAB

Another trick for stalking the unknown self is to picture your parents' psychological undergrounds. The fears, forbidden possibilities, and inconceivable alternatives of one generation are passed on in unspoken form to the next. Verbal preachments are not a part of the psychological underground: if you remember your mother saying, "A nice little girl doesn't stand on her head with a dress on," that is not an aspect of your unknown self. The nonverbal messages were transmitted in unconscious ways and are usually messages that your parents would deny having sent. Ask your ultra-masculine father if he taught you that women are frightening enemies to be conquered and kept at a distance and he will likely deny it. Ask your anxious mother if she taught you never to be satisfied and she won't know where you got such an idea. Nevertheless, the messages were sent and received, in actions if not in words.

- What horrified your parents? What made them scold you?
- What topics of conversation were forbidden? How did you know they were?
- What ways of life or habits were out of the question?
- What do you think your father and mother never did?

The Devil's Chariot

I am not: worrisome, inaccessible, romantic, idealistic, addicted to dope, manipulative, a performer, inarticulate, inattentive, or silly.

Or am I? I can take it easy with the best of them, but somewhere under my blithe spirit I do worry a lot about losing my center, being too open, getting closed down due to overexposure. There are a lot of mysterious things in myself that I don't want to give to people, hidden places which I only let a few chosen people see. . . . I'm really much less accessible than I pretend to be. But my romantic ideal, the self-portrait I carry around in my mind, has no tolerance for inaccessibility. The perfect me is always open to people and information. When I'm feeling really high I do take a lot in, but every so often that ideal gives way. Then I accuse myself of being narrow and stunted, of blocking out the world. . . . I guess that's where dope comes in. I'm addicted to being high, cruising at my own speed. People often criticize me for chasing highs, but I hate to feel hassled or crowded and marijuana is a nice tranquilizer. It helps me slow down and draw life in. It shuts out all those race-track mind-trips where everybody leaves the starting gate at once instead of just letting the horse gallop on his own time. . . . I'm also pretty manipulative. I have a way of pretending to let things happen when actually I'm making them happen the way I want them to. It's like memorizing a recipe, filling the cupboard, and then pretending to cook by feel—a little of this, a little of that, and presto! A perfect pie! . . . That's tied into being a performer. As a musician (and otherwise) I use all the tricks I can to pull off the response I need from a person or a group. It goes with my need to be smooth, to do things with style. I pull off a lot of good performances, but they're less spontaneous than they seem because of my need to come off well.

I also have a way of speeding ahead or jumping backward and missing what's happening right in front of me, especially where words are concerned. I think I'm articulate, but it takes so much energy to translate and hang onto words that often I just withdraw, leave my body sitting there, and turn

Woman, in the picture language of mythology, represents the totality of what can be known. The hero is the one who comes to know.
JOSEPH CAMPBELL,
Hero with a Thousand Faces

And the Lord God commanded the man, saying, "You may freely eat of every tree of the garden; but of the tree of the knowledge of good and evil you shall not eat, for in the day that you eat of it you shall die." . . . But the serpent said to the woman, "You will not die. For God knows that when you eat of it your eyes will be opened, and you will be like God, knowing good and evil."
Genesis

inward. When I come back I find myself in the center of a conversation with somebody stranded on the other end. . . . Okay, yeah, I'm silly too sometimes. I act that way in order to slip out of awkward situations. It hurts to think of myself as silly. It's like dumb-blondness, a misfire, throwing away all your experience. I dislike myself when I'm too stupid to see what I'm doing.

The other night all my negatives ganged up on me. I'd been doing a lot of things for weeks without admitting that they were hurting me, but they were. I dragged my guitar and a pint of tequila to a friend's house downtown across from a mortuary. I was wailing blues out the window, trying to drown my depression in music, but this time it didn't work. I sank lower and lower, still denying the stupid things I was doing to myself. So finally I got in my car, rolled up the windows, turned on the radio, and sped along the freeway at 70 miles an hour. No one could come in, my defenses were safe in my steel cocoon. I felt so sick I could hardly drive. The freeway signs would read "next exit ¼ mile" and then it would not appear. It was terrible, thrashing around on all that hard concrete, whizzing right past bushes and grass and sky on the Devil's Chariot. I didn't want to stop to look at the dead thing that was trying to be born in me. I was using the freeway like a whip, trying to make a fast getaway: fill my head with noise, jump in my Chevy (the antithetical horse), and ride off to nowhere forever! It was stupid. As soon as I stopped I knew it. That's when I turned around, went to a friend's house, and cried my way back to a more natural, positive place.

—LIZA is a young, footloose musician

BODYMIND

And the Word became flesh and dwelt among us, full of grace and truth.
The Gospel According to John

Our language, like a practiced magician, tricks us into believing in the existence of two separate entities called mind and body. Mind/body language reflects a persistent schizophrenic experience of the self, a dualism present in most civilized cultures. In Greek experience it was reflected in the dichotomy between soul and body, in Christianity in the warfare between spirit and flesh, in Victorian society in the tension between reason and emotion. We currently find it in the professional separation of physical and psychological medicine. It also occurs in the romantic idea that a person can superimpose a civilized mind dedicated to the virtues of work, reason, and control on a free, sensual body.

If we were fully integrated persons we might refer to ourselves as *being* bodyminds rather than as *having* bodies. We bring our whole selves—complete with autobiography—to every act of thinking or sensing. Eyes, ears, noses, mouths, genitals, and brains are all affected by history and politics.

The split between our bodies and our minds has a certain conservative survival value: so long as we *have* bodies we can deal with them as if they were possessions that we can manipulate or machines that can be repaired by experts when they break down.

It's comforting to believe that something (mind, soul, spirit) survives the death of the body. But to be fully thoughtful and sensuous is to be fully mortal. Death and sensuality belong together. Either/or dichotomies split us off from the erotic possibilities of personal integration. Mental and sensory awakenings are in no way mutually exclusive. If coming to our senses means losing our minds, it's a questionable trade. Brains and toes and bellies are all erogenous zones, and who wants to lose one of those? The trick is to learn to be fully present in the world.

Viewpoints

- Take a large piece of paper and an assortment of colored pencils or crayons and draw a picture of yourself in any way you want. It might be symbolic or literal, clothed or nude, a portrait or a full figure.
- Stop. If you plan to take this trip, do the above before reading further.

You are a body in a given time and place. The way you experience your body reflects your view of exis-

What we call "I" is just a swinging door which moves when we inhale and when we exhale.
SHUNRYU SUZUKI,
Zen Mind, Beginner's Mind

Myth is a manifestation in symbolic images, in metaphorical images, of the energies of the organs of the body in conflict with each other. This organ wants this, that organ wants that. The brain is one of the organs.
JOSEPH CAMPBELL,
The Power of Myth

To the enlightened man, however, whose consciousness embraces the universe, to him the universe becomes his "body."
LAMA ANAGARIKA
GOVINDA

tence. Assume that the paper on which you just drew yourself is the world. What does your body image tell you about your world?

- Do you fill all or part of your space?
- How realistic or symbolic is your representation of yourself?
- Is your outline sharp, fuzzy, disconnected, flowing?
- Is your figure open or closed?
- What parts of your body are missing? Out of proportion? Hidden?
- Are you clothed or nude? Is your body designed to be seen? Touched?
- What colors predominate?
- Give your drawing a name. What mythical (fairy tale, movie, television, storybook) character does it bring to mind?

The body is the spirit incognito. The human spirit and body are belly to belly with the cosmos. Or as the old mystics said: as below, so above; deeper in is further out; the microcosm reflects the macrocosm.
SANDOR McNAB

It's not easy to keep track of all the parts of your body. There usually is a difference between what you think you feel and what you actually feel. Create a feeling map of the lively and sluggish areas of your body. Lie quietly in a comfortable position and focus your attention on your toes, insteps, ankles, and on up on all sides until you have traveled over your entire body.

- Where do you feel numb, tense, warm, electric, heavy, constricted, relaxed?
- When you locate a part of your body that is numb or hurting, take a trip inside, try to find out why. See if there's anything you can do to relax it or make it feel better.

FRIENDLY EYES OR DEADLY WATCHERS

The eyes have it. We are lookers. Of the many possible ways of knowing, many of us (introverts and shy people, at least) prefer the mode that lets us watch, keeps us spectators. From a distance it's easier to observe, to discern forms and patterns, and to categorize. When we neglect our other senses it is hard to imagine what it might be like to perceive the world through smell, taste, sound, or touch. By definition, we can't see what it would be like to feel any other way.

The eyes may be used to observe or to caress, to keep a safe distance or to pull things closer to us. But when the eyes dominate, the more intimate senses may be neglected. Instead of touching we examine and judge. We become passive spectators, distant from the world, watchers not responsible for what occurs. Then our passivity makes us victims rather than initiators.

Self-consciousness and paranoia are the results of hyperobjectivity and self-criticism. In self-consciousness the I watches rather than acts. In paranoia the eyes are projected onto an enemy—"they are watching me."

The spectator stance is rooted in childhood. In infancy we were watched over. The omniscient eyes of parents bathed us in smiles (maybe) and fended off hot stoves, barking dogs, and strangers. But the caring eyes also were prying, seeing around and through us. We were secure but transparent. In time we wanted freedom enough to dare secrecy. In hideaways under weeping willows, or behind cellar doors, we gained self-knowledge and shame. When we played I'll-show-you-mine-if-you-will-show-me-yours we found that self-consciousness shadows the steps of each new freedom.

But the judging eyes were not easily escaped. The watchdogs of social morality warned us that God could see where parents could not, and conscience (the internalized eyes) reminded us when we were doing anything bad, mad, or dangerous. Thus, conscience made watchers of us all. For most of us, growing up meant transferring the authority from parental and divine eyes to those of society—teachers, bosses, mates, review boards, neighbors, and police. The eyes were everywhere.

When the woman saw that the tree was to be desired to make one wise, she took of its fruit and ate; and she also gave some to her husband, and he ate. Then the eyes of both were opened, and they knew that they were naked; and they sewed fig leaves together and made themselves aprons. And they heard the sound of the Lord God walking in the garden in the cool of the day, and the man and his wife hid themselves from the presence of the Lord God among the trees of the garden.
Genesis

Conscience doth make cowards of us all.
WILLIAM SHAKESPEARE

Pure spontaneity—freedom from all watchers—is rare, but it is possible to mitigate self-consciousness. One good way to begin is by recovering the use of our other senses. Once we remove from our eyes and brains the pressure to control, the other senses are free to receive.

Viewpoints

Eyes can do many things. They may be hard or soft, focused or unfocused, penetrating or caressing, dull or sparkling, darting or open. Change the eye that sees and you change the world that is seen. What is the relationship between your feelings about the world and the way you use your eyes?

- Open and close your eyes for several minutes. Each time you close them tighten and squeeze your eye muscles. When you open your eyes, relax. Continue until you feel your vision blur and soften. Notice how your peripheral vision increases as sharpness of focus decreases. What happens to your other senses when you see the world through a soft haze?
- When you are in a public place, watch eyes. Observe the stories being told by challenging looks, furtive glances, intense concentration. Notice where eyes focus and where they don't. Where are public eyes forbidden to linger? (Try staring at someone's sausage in a restaurant!)

Identifying the eyes you imagine are watching and judging you is one way to move beyond self-consciousness to greater spontaneity.

- When were you first aware of being watched?
- Who is watching you now?
- For what imagined audience do you perform? Dress? Work? Create? Make love?
- What look is most often in the eyes of your

watchers? Do your actions please them or do they disapprove? Of what are you proud or ashamed when you imagine that X is watching you?

- When you are most self-conscious and self-critical, what ideal are you chasing?
- If you weren't busy watching yourself, what would you do?

The Trouble with Maraschino Cherries

As a kid I was sure that my father saw every move I made. Even though he apparently had only two eyes, he always seemed to catch my slightest slip-up. One day he lined up his five children in the kitchen and demanded a confession from the one who ate the maraschino cherries. I said I didn't do it, but then he made us stick out our tongues and sure enough, there was mine pink as a third-degree burn. He spanked me twice that time: once for lying and once for snitching the cherries.

I learned to outfox my father by doing most of my trespassing outside the house. But then I discovered God, and I was trapped again. God had some really rigid puritanical ideas like, "Whosoever looks at a woman with lust in his heart has sinned . . ." and, since I figured that went for girls too, I was worried. It was no longer good enough to hide or minimize my weaknesses: now I had to be pure to the core. God was probably nowhere around, but His witnesses tricked me into the habit of watching myself with the eyes of a slavemaster!

By the time I was sixteen and sexy I was looking up to my older sister instead of Jesus. I thought she was wild and beautiful and brave, and I wanted to be like her but didn't quite dare. God and my father were still casting their little shadows over me, frowning at my excesses. So I was stuck in limbo. I had the feeling that my sister also was watching me now, and over and over again I imagined her disappointment at my cowardice. For years I carried her around in my mind like a tiny Buddha, sitting in the corner silently watching, appearing and disappearing. When I married

Conscience is what Freud in his later writings called the super-ego; which in earlier writings he more eloquently called the "watching institution." The construction of the super-ego moves the open-air theater indoors. Action . . . is now displayed to an internal observer; a super-ego looking down from above; the god in the gallery, watching his children play.
N. O. BROWN,
Love's Body

before I was really ready she seemed disappointed and distant. When I chased after random good graces she seemed to be laughing at me. Whenever I backed myself into a sharp corner she pointed to an opposite possibility and I felt torn in two.

Then, gradually, I learned the amazing truth: I am my own worst watcher. Half the time I watch myself like a cool, distant audience checking for grace, humor, passion, accuracy, and spontaneity in every action! Other times I jump behind the eyes of someone specific—waitress, cab driver, enemy—and look over at myself the way the others used to do. These watchers are always equipped with stern and perfect vision. If I see them seeing me acting foolish or vulnerable in any way I feel suddenly appalled, and withdraw from whatever's happening. Those sickening moments I leave my friends (over there with *her*, acting like asses!) in the lurch.

More than anything else in the world I want to learn to *feel* myself from the inside rather than *watch* myself from the outside with that mean set of eyes. Lately I've had some new experiences of absolute self-acceptance: suddenly I am my own best friend and anything I do or feel is all right. Eye strain and migraines dissolve, and I feel euphoric toward everything around me. It's like discovering an air pocket in a hurricane.

—VALERIE works as a legal secretary

I Samuel XVI, 7: "For Jehovah seeth not as a man seeth; for man looketh on the outward appearance, but Jehovah looketh on the heart." Christian virtue is displayed to an even more exacting audience than Stoic conscience. . . . Christianity will not be rid of the performance principle . . . until it gets rid of the spectre of the Father, Old Noboddaddy, the watching institution.
N. O. BROWN,
Love's Body

SEX: WHAT IS IT WE REALLY WANT?

For a while in the 1960s and 1970s, the idea of free love became a kind of cultural temptation for mainstream America. Snug in our cinema seats we watched *Bob and Carol and Ted and Alice* hop in and out of bed together in a comic attempt to enliven their marriages by changing partners. In those years we saw a common domestic unrest and a rash of divorces: droves of newly liberated men and women set out to play the field; still others stayed together for the kids and had affairs, or dreamed about them. It looked for a time as if free love and the resultant dissolution of the American family would play a major role in the downfall of Western civilization.

Singles bars sprang up in cities, quickly becoming places where people gathered to shop for sex partners. *Looking for Mr. Goodbar* hit the silver screen with the terrible message that free love wasn't so free after all: beyond the fear of sexually transmitted diseases and persistent loneliness, we were saddled with the gruesome specter of a psychotic killer leaving a bar with a good Catholic girl and taking her on her last free ride. Despite the romantic stories and screenplays we'd been raised on, we were beginning to learn that attraction and happiness, like sex and intimacy, did not necessarily go hand and hand.

Johnny Lee's rendition of the country-western song "Looking for Love" ("Looking for love in all the wrong places/looking for love in too many faces/ searching your eyes/looking for traces of what I'm dreaming of . . ."), which topped the record charts in the early 1980s, describes a gradual, collective turn away from disembodied sex and back toward relationship. Now the outbreak of AIDS has sounded the death knell of free love. Many of us still believe in love, but we're gun-shy: after a string of broken vows how are we to know what is love and what is only lust?

Why is sex such a thorny issue for human beings? The birds and the bees do it naturally by the numbers and the seasons, but human beings, as cultural animals, are compelled to interpret, symbolize, and mythologize the major biological acts of existence—birth, death, eating, excreting, sleeping, and sex. Long ago we defined masculinity and femininity by social and economic roles and agreed to live accordingly. Today, in the age of information and nuclear blast, our sense of what we are and why we are here has been drastically altered.

Our times have thrown our social and sexual contracts into an uproar. If the books and movies of this decade—for example, *Kramer vs. Kramer, An Unmarried*

Then the Lord God said, "It is not good that the man should be alone". . . . So the Lord God caused a deep sleep to fall upon the man, and while he slept took one of his ribs and closed up its place with flesh; and the rib which the Lord God had taken from the man he made into a woman and brought her to the man. Then the man said, "This at last is bone of my bone and flesh of my flesh; she shall be called Woman because she was taken out of Man." . . . And the man and his wife were both naked, and were not ashamed.
Genesis

*The moment I heard my
first love story
I started looking for
you, not knowing
how blind that was.
Lovers don't finally meet
somewhere.
They're in each other all
along.*
RUMI

*As Adam, early in the
    morning,
Walking forth from the
    bower, refresh'd with
    sleep;
Behold me where I
    pass—hear my voice—
    approach,
Touch me—touch the
    palm of your hand to
    my Body as I pass;
Be not afraid of my
    Body.*
WALT WHITMAN,
*"As Adam, Early in the
Morning"*

Woman, The Good Mother, Fatal Attraction—are telling us that mating for life is an outdated phenomenon, still there exists within us a powerful urge to couple, to reunite with our platonic other half, to complete our journey through this life with the one we love. How are we to reconcile our (perhaps fatal) attraction to life in the fast lane with our private longing for intimate love?

By calling into question traditional Western ideas of womanhood, manhood, parenthood, and the institution of marriage as the officially sanctioned place for sexual coupling, the sexual revolution has cast us into chaos and pain but also shows us a way to get through. The way out, it seems, is to look within. Thus we can seek to become whole persons.

Societal schisms between masculine and feminine reflect a commensurate duality in the self. Every man has a tender, nurturing, dark, and emotional side to him (some call this "feminine"), just as every questing woman will somewhere find shining in herself a logical, penetrant, bright light (dubbed "masculine" by some). By looking inward we will recognize ourselves at our best and worst; by integrating the male and female parts of ourselves we can hope to accept or reject potential partners from the depths of our self-knowledge.

When all is said and done, it may well be that adult human sexual longing is not a quest for pleasure and variety, but a search for intimacy. Who doesn't long for the so-called other, whose presence relaxes you into yourself, who allows you to stop searching and come home to your multiple selves? Johnny Lee's cowboy "looking for love" sings: "Now that I've found a friend and a lover/ I bless the day I discovered/ another heart/ looking for love." We might take these lyrics as a general prescription for success in sexual love: turn from searching outward to looking into your own heart, for when you know your heart, your counterpart—the one who mirrors your deepest desires—may prove close at hand.

Viewpoints

Traditionally, masculine and feminine characteristics and virtues have been juxtaposed:

Feminine	Masculine
passive	active, aggressive
soft	hard
nurturing	protecting
patient	insistent
welcoming	penetrating
oriented toward the private sphere of home, family, and children	oriented toward the public sphere of politics, and war
symbolized by the left hand, darkness, the moon	symbolized by the right hand, light, the sun
governed by emotion, hence mysterious and dangerous	governed by reason, hence responsible
submissive	dominant
inferior	superior

- How much has your self-image been shaped by these stereotyped notions and roles?
- Tell the story of how you learned what a woman or man was supposed to want and be.
- How satisfied or frustrated are you with the current standards of sexuality? With your own sexuality?
- If you could change places with your mate or lover, what would be the easiest and hardest aspects of your new roles? What changes would you make in your relationship?

The degree and kind of a person's sexuality reaches up into the topmost summit of his spirit.
FRIEDRICH NIETZSCHE

Your body contains both male and female hormones just as your psyche includes developed images of the ideal male and female. By looking at men and women you admire and desire, masculine and feminine figures in your dreams, you will get an idea of your own sexual archetypes.

- How do you experience the masculine characteristics and feminine characteristics in yourself?
- Develop a dialogue between the man and the woman within you. Let them talk to each other. How does the feminine side of your personality relate to the masculine side? How does the man in you want to be loved by the woman?
- Take yourself on a fantasy trip in which your masculine and feminine parts are all sexually satisfied.

Necessary, forever necessary, to burn out false shames and smelt the heaviest ore of the body into purity.
D. H. LAWRENCE

Try some new sexual languages. Experiment with changing the words you use. What happens?

Myths are frequently created to explain why there are two sexes and a variety of sexual preference. In Genesis, Eve was liberated from Adam's rib so that man could have a companion. Plato said that people were once joined back to back—woman-woman, man-man, man-woman, until finally the gods took compassion and split them down the middle so they could face each other and make love.

- Make up your own myth about the origin of sexes. Or redesign them altogether (try a world with one sex, or four).

The Invisible Home Run

It is fatal to be a man or woman pure and simple; one must be woman-manly or man-womanly.
VIRGINIA WOOLF,
A Room of One's Own

When I was twelve, I wanted to be a boy in the worst way. I played great baseball and dreamed of joining the school team but I knew they'd never let me, so I put on a T-shirt to show my flat chest and applied for bat boy. One afternoon they let me do it but then the girls came and pulled my cap off and my hair fell down and everyone laughed. That was the end of that.

In the eighth grade I was crazy to be a sports announcer since I couldn't play professionally myself. I painted stripes on a beer bottle, turned it upside down, and announced all the plays from the top of the bleachers. I was obsessed. But one day it hit me that the whole dream was futile—the world would never accept me as a sports announcer—so after everyone left the field I went down, slugged an invisible home run, jogged around the bases, and walked slowly home. At that moment I lost all interest in baseball and haven't watched a single game since.

At seventeen I still didn't have any breasts—not the slightest sign of them. All my boyfriends turned out to be friends. I practiced kissing the bathroom mirror and saying "yes," but nothing happened. I was sure that God was punishing me for shunning my femininity for so long. Finally my mother took me to a doctor who gave me some hormone shots and a few long weeks later I was profusely bleeding and budding. I was hugely relieved, but still I felt like a fake for needing so much help just to become a woman.

By now it's clear to me that nobody's got it made. The feminine personality feels to me essentially sturdy, self-aware, remorseful, dependent, confused, frivolous, self-deprecating, emotional, and bored. Men are generally block-ish, competitive, hostile, arrogant, aggressive, emotionally bottled, articulate, and vulnerable. The male stance essentially says, "I am what I am," while the female sends a lot of double messages (just look at our eyes—one eye dropping a tear, and the other painted for seduction!). But in order to support their artificial superiority men have to be constantly equipped to do battle, and they end up lying to themselves a lot to disguise the tender feelings which get in the way. At the core I feel mostly feminine and soft and proud but sometimes I wish I had more courage. On the other hand, their physiology makes men vulnerable in a way that women aren't. When the penis goes limp at the wrong time (and who's got remote control?) a man gets wiped out. The same thing happens to women, of course, but it's not so obvious. Women are able to keep up two faces, but at the same time we get stagnant and bored because we're not *forced* to act in the outside world.

If I'd been born a man I'm sure I'd have twice the amount of money, job status, and worldly confidence that I have

In the embrace of his beloved a man forgets the whole world; everything within and without. In the very same way, he who embraces the Self knows neither within or without.
BRIHADARANYAKA
UPANISHAD

The moderns, men and women of passion, expect irresistible love to produce some revelation either regarding themselves or about life at large. This is a last vestige of primitive mysticism. . . . Passion is everywhere treated as an experience, something that will alter my life and enrich it with the unexpected, with thrilling chances, and with enjoyment ever more violent and gratifying.
DENIS DE ROUGEMONT,
Love in the Western World

now. Of course I'd also lose my easy access to men with power (they take you places for show, or make love to you as if you were a goddess) but it would be worth it. I'd be a human being and people (men especially) would listen to me, respect me, maybe even like me for once! As a man I hope I'd be confident enough to enjoy women—especially strong ones—and not fall into treating them like dumb passive playthings.

Sexually, the major change in my behavior would concern seductions. Most men have no idea what power there is in gentleness: they handle footballs and hammers more sensitively than a human body. As a man (probably in love with a woman like me!) I could afford to be a deeply attentive lover, since I'd know that women castrate when they feel cheated or overlooked, not because they are natural-born bitches.

—FRANCIS is a professional researcher who was active in the Civil Rights Movement

TIME FRAMES: WHERE IS NOW?

To every thing there is a season, and a time to every purpose under heaven: A time to be born, and a time to die; a time to plant, and a time to pluck up that which is planted; a time to kill, and a time to heal; . . . A time to weep, and a time to laugh; . . . A time to keep silence, and a time to speak; a time to love, and a time to hate; a time of war, and a time of peace.
Ecclesiastes

What's happening? What's going on now? Where in the world are we? If only we could hook up a metacomputer to an omniscient sensing device we could, in theory, create a machine that would give us an accurate readout on the exact placement of every particle in the universe at this precise moment. And then we would know what's happening at this point in time.

But this moment and the meaning of this moment—fact and interpretation—are not separable. Human beings inevitably are philosophical animals. We interpret, discover, and create meaning in the act of perception. We think with our senses, see with our hearts, and feel with our brains. We use images, analogies, and metaphors to understand the world around us and the meaning of life as a whole. We live within a framework that gives meaning to our experience. The philosophical context within which we live determines the way we perceive the content of our days. G. K. Chesterton had a sense of this when he advised landlords to inquire after a potential tenant's philosophy of life rather than his financial affairs. A man who constantly feels the pressure of time running out just might run out himself.

The history of religion and philosophy provides a handy exhibit of images and analogies that can be used to frame experience. Each worldview embodies a philosophy of time that gives meaning to the present moment. What's happening always depends on a myth or metaphor that explains why anything is happening:

If the world is an artifact shaped by a divine craftsman (Plato), then time is the moving image of eternity and this moment should be used for contemplating the eternal forms and making things in the world conform to them.

If the world is a battleground on which the forces of evil have nearly defeated the forces of goodness (Gnosticism, Manicheanism), then time is a prison that keeps man's spirit locked into matter and this moment should be used for escape.

If the world is a material illusion in an eternal sea of nothingness (Buddhism), then time is a dream and this moment is for enlightenment, awakening from illusion.

If the world is the arena God has assigned to His free creatures (Christianity), then time is an opportunity for freedom and the present moment may be used for deciding, creating, and enjoying.

If the world is a happenstance conjunction of erratic atoms (atheistic existentialism), then time is unbridled chaos and it doesn't matter what you do with the present moment.

If the world is a mystery to be savored, and used responsibly but never explained (mysticism), then time is the filter through which the human animal perceives the mystery of being, and now is a strange gift that will never come again.

If the world is an immense organism that is dying and being reborn like a plant (cosmic, maternal religions, Nietzsche), then time is a recurring cycle and this moment is not new and may occur again and again.

Religious man experiences two kinds of time—profane and sacred. The one is an evanescent duration, the other a "succession of eternities," periodically recoverable during the festivals that made up the sacred calendar. The liturgical time of the calendar flows in a closed circle; it is the cosmic time of the year, sanctified by the works of the gods.
MIRCEA ELIADE,
The Sacred and the Profane

If the world is a place where only the fit survive (evolutionary capitalism), then time is money and this moment should be used productively to better oneself in the competition . . .

Time is money.
BENJAMIN FRANKLIN

Many of us have no such systematic philosophies in which to frame our understanding of time so we make do with more modest images, intuitions, or feelings. Time is an old gypsy, or a snake that swallows its own tail. It is for killing or filling, using or keeping track of, or improving. When we suspect that time is running down (the golden ages are all in the past; glory is gone with childhood) we face our accumulating years with dread of decay. In more buoyant moments when time seems to be moving toward fulfillment (the New Jerusalem, or maturity), we feel the years mellowing us like fine wine. However modest or elaborate our principles of interpretation may be, they are sure to be homogenized into the way we experience this passing moment.

Viewpoints

Time is the moving image of eternity.
PLATO

Your time shows your limits. Whether you believe in reincarnation or the finality of death, in cyclical or linear time, this moment is in the context of a larger picture. Draw a life-map, a diagram, a chart, or a timeline that will point to where you are now.

- How much time have you spent? How much is left?
- Do you like the way you've spent your time so far?
- Have you been here before? Will you be here again?
- Where are you going? Where have you come from?
- What is the meaning of time for you? Are you on the road to somewhere, do you want to be going, is where you are now all right with you?

An Imaginary Line

I started out drawing my life-map in good spirits and ended up feeling foul: instead of picturing a meandering road or an open space bubbled with galaxies or something fluid, I turn out a regular progress graph! It's that damn straight line down the center that holds me accountable, always judging me in terms of how high I leap or how low I sink. And to make it worse, so few of the jags ever really get off the ground. . . .

I suppose my high/low graphing system got set up way back when I was a kid. I was a skinny little guy with red hair and slow-motion responses and an older sister who grabbed up all the attention. My childhood wasn't particularly traumatic, it was just low on *triumphs:* it's as if I walked around in continual low-level anxiety, all the time hugging an imaginary line. Things that happened infrequently, or experiences that were too good or too spooky to believe, just didn't register with me, which is probably why so much subtlety and richness got left off my map.

In college things picked up some, but then I joined the Marines and disengaged again. For three years my body went through active maneuvers while my mind stayed aloof. I ruminated a lot, chewing the cud of past experiences, and refused to accept what was going on around me as very real or relevant. I was a Marine fighting in Vietnam but it hardly registered; even now it's hard to believe I was there. My Lais probably happen that way: people just don't bother to *be there* and so they don't make distinctions between shooting at targets and shooting at soldiers, between shooting at people and shooting at babies.

After graduate school I got really excited about my work, which then shot me into an even higher wave of political activism. At the peak of all that I fell in love and was feeling really fantastic, but I guess I wasn't going to escape the straight line that easily. . . . All of a sudden there was a tragedy on the other side of the country and my marriage celebration was postponed and everything caved in at once, like a parachute hitting ground. After that I hobbled along the old line for a long time, feeling generally anxious and negative. It's only recently—since my move to another town—that I finally seem to be getting recharged.

As a matter of fact, my graph does show something new happening. Instead of a median line chewed up by little saw teeth it looks like I'm beginning to ride rhythmic waves: high energy and excitement at the crest, low energy and

It was a fine feeling that made the spirit of the Greek language signify chronos, *"formal time,"* with a different word from kairos, *"the right time". . . . The consciousness of the* kairos *is dependent on one's being inwardly grasped by the fate and destiny of the time. Kairos is every turning point in history in which the eternal judges and transforms the temporal.*
PAUL TILLICH,
The Protestant Era

For Judaism, time has a beginning and will have an end. The idea of cyclic time is left behind. Yahweh no longer manifests himself in cosmic time *(like the gods of other religions) but in a* historical time, *which is irreversible.*
MIRCEA ELIADE,
The Sacred and the Profane

relaxation in the trough. When I look at my life that way I don't have to box it up or kill the past off with retrospective judgments. If my life's a wave, then there's no pass or fail, just the building and falling and building. That means I don't have to invent a superman to live up to or a nebish to live down.

So right now I'm sliding down the back of a six-month high into a low pocket, getting ready to digest and ruminate before starting up a new front of excitation or risk-taking of some sort. If this last hill represents a trend, then my wave-curves are definitely getting smoother and the space between them is lengthening, all of which is reflected in the fact that my feelings are thawing out. Hopefully this mellowing process will continue so that the wave amplitude peaks when I'm about fifty, stays high for a while, and then very gradually tapers down until at some point I just stop living. I'm not young enough any more to be interested in those sharp roller-coaster curves where every day's a whole new goddamn turning point. But I do look forward to deepening involvements and periodic rest and nice smooth wave-sets rolling into the future.

—NED is a free-lance journalist

To tell a myth is to proclaim what happened ab origine. . . . We must do what the Gods did in the beginning. . . . One becomes truly a man only by conforming to the teaching of the myths, that is, by imitating the gods.
MIRCEA ELIADE,
The Sacred and the Profane

4

THE PAST

It's Still Happening

We love the present tense. Be here *now*. Yesterday is gone and best forgotten; our tradition is to have no tradition. We aren't Europeans buried in ancient tombs and cathedrals and medieval ruins. We were born yesterday and we will be young forever. Over thirty is over the bridge. Age embarrasses us; remembrance is a function of senility. We exile the aged to Sun City leper colonies so they won't impair our illusion of endless summer.

But history is not so easily dismissed. Repressed memories, national or personal, won't stay down. To be alive is to have a past. Our only choice is whether we will repress or re-create the past. Childhood may be distant, but it is never quite lost; as full-grown men and women we carry tiny laughing and whimpering children around inside us. We either repress the past and continue to fight its wars with new personnel or we invite it into awareness so that we may see how it has shaped the present.

History is bunk.
HENRY FORD

The moment you begin to tell your stories you may find that memory is a trickster who picks and chooses scenes. What happened to you in the past has yet to be determined. Ninety-nine times you tell the story of the day you were whipped for stealing apples you didn't steal. Then, in the hundredth telling, you remember that you *did* steal them and the whole scene changes. Your memories of what happened to you in 1953 will be different in 1975, and again in the year 2000.

A people without history is like the wind on the buffalo grass.
Sioux proverb

I had a terribly strong attachment to my personal history. My family roots were deep. I honestly felt that without them my life had no continuity or purpose. . . . I don't have personal history anymore. . . . I dropped it one day when I felt it was no longer necessary.
DON JUAN,
Journey to Ixtlan

Both national histories and individual autobiographies are passional accounts of the past. They are not a collection of objective facts but stories constructed to prove some point. History is more like myth than science in that it justifies some present custom or value.

The past is open to revision because memory is a function of present intention. History is always constructed to prove some point. If you were a poor abused child, a victim of parents and circumstances, you probably will continue to be a victim. If as a child you chose your responses to people and surroundings you probably will continue to be a free agent. You probably will discover in your future about as much freedom as you can find in your past.

The following pages suggest ways that you can turn your story over (and over) and find new perspectives on past events and emotions. You may invent a new past and open up a novel future.

CLAN AND FAMILY

We are obliged to repeat what we cannot remember. This world is repetition-compulsion, is karma: the burden of the past, a future determined by the past, causality. This world is dreams, the present transformed into the past, the shadow of the past falling on the present. The awakening explodes the cave of shadows; it is the end of the world.
N. O. BROWN,
Love's Body

Every person is plural. There is no *I* without *we*. Each of us was shaped by a social group. To know yourself is to understand your people. There is no psychology without sociology.

Every family has rules, customs, mores, traditions, taboos, rituals, and habitual ways of interacting that shape and shade the personality of each member. Your individual story is set within a framework of family history.

Viewpoints

Who are you? Where did you come from? Who are your people? Detail stimulates memory. By recapturing specific events and scenes from your past, you can trace a thread of detail from the known into the unknown. Reconstruct the physical setting of your childhood and you may recover the flavor of the family in which your psyche was first marinated.

- Draw a detailed floor plan of a house you lived in before you were ten.
- As you enter each room imagine the furniture, pictures, smells, and events you associate with the room.
- Where were your secret places? (Where did you stash your comic books or go when you wanted to be alone?)
- Who lived in the house with you?
- What was the dominant mood in the household?
- Which rooms are you unable to reconstruct in memory? Why do you think you forgot them?
- Are there rooms you can't enter?

After you've filled in as much detail as you can remember, take someone on a tour of your house. Describe it as a novelist would so that your listener can feel the texture of the couch you lay on when you were sick, smell the bread baking, feel the emotions that permeated the house.

If you are playing with these Viewpoints in a group, use several persons to create a living sculpture of your family. Or pose your family members in an imaginary photograph that would represent their relative positions.

- What position did each member occupy?
- Are your parents facing each other, going in opposite directions, on the same level? Are they supportive or antagonistic? Who is leaning on whom?
- Which members are close to each other and which are distant? Where is the center of the family?
- What are the basic bonds and jealousies among the siblings?
- Who is trying to get away from the family?

Generally speaking, all the life which the parents could have lived, but of which they thwarted themselves for artificial motives, is passed on to the children in substitute form. . . . The children are driven unconsciously in a direction that is intended to compensate for everything that was left unfulfilled in the lives of their parents.
C. G. JUNG,
The Portable Jung

The Palace

I lived with my mother, father, and little brother in the same house for twenty years. The others are still there. The rooms are always filled with fresh-cut flowers and colorful paintings. The furniture is tasteful and the house is handsome, but underneath it something is uneasy. I think I grew up in its image.

As long as I can remember, my mother's been queen of the palace. This should have made royalty of the rest of us but it didn't work that way. Mother shuffled us like face cards in a marked deck. To live in the house we signed a contract to play by her rules.

I think of the house in four sections. My room, Daniel's room, and Dad's study are outposts surrounding the kitchen. Daniel spends most of his life upstairs in his room with electric trains and microscopes and scrap metal. Dad's desk sits in a nook behind the staircase downstairs. Although no one will admit it, the den is rarely used for anything but storage, so Dad can sit there undisturbed, paying his bills.

My room is on the bottom floor at the end of a long cold hallway, cavelike, but full of its own sunshine. It was my sanctuary, and I felt uneasy when the others came down there. Mom and Dad owned the walls, but I plastered them over, inch by inch, with photographs and lovely paintings (mine)—pictures from my imagination. The bookshelves were another barricade against my parents and their world. Neither of them read much, so the books symbolized my separateness.

On winter afternoons Dan and I used to sit at the dining-room table with our homework. The dining room opens into the kitchen where Mother was inevitably puttering and keeping a protective eye on us. The kitchen was her special kingdom: the refrigerator a treasure chest, the sink a well, the TV a music box.

Dinnertime was crucial. Everyone had to be presentable and prompt. The whole thing is unpleasant to think about mostly because at Mom's dinner table I felt like a second-class citizen. Dad always said his piece first: what happened at the office, family decisions to be made, *et cetera*. Then there would be some political argument, arrogant bullshit

Time present and time past
Are both perhaps present in time future
And time future contained in time past.
T. S. ELIOT

The psyche is not of today; its ancestry goes back many millions of years. Individual consciousness is only the flower and the fruit of a season.
C. G. JUNG,
The Portable Jung

all around, me struggling to overpower Dad, hoping to prove my first-class status. But Mom protected him. She set him up as head of the royal family, although we all knew it was she who really ruled.

My parents' bedroom is the only room I left out of the drawing. It falls off the left edge of the page. I guess that's because it's their exclusive territory, the place where they make love and plot together. What that area of the house meant to me was a full-length mirror and a heated bathroom. I used the mirror when no one was around, but the bathroom was a constant sore spot. Mother used it as a power tool, jealously guarding the hot water in case Dad should suddenly want a shower in the middle of the afternoon! My basement bathroom was cold and uncomfortable but theirs was taboo for me unless Dad was out of town.

Mom has always guarded Dad's space. They married when Mom and I escaped from wartime Germany. I was five then. I think maybe her protectiveness toward him was a compensation for her fierce attachment to me: I was all that was left of her family. Anyhow, she trained me (and later Daniel) not to talk back to our father. She said that she could "take it and bear it" but that he "deserved respect"— which made him seem ridiculously fragile.

So the queen was also the sacrificial lamb. Mom always let us know what motherhood cost her in dollars and pain, and we felt appropriately guilty. I began to see the price I paid to live in that privileged kingdom. In exchange for being a good girl (finishing college, looking lovely, holding down jobs I didn't like, vacationing with the family) I received money and food and praise. But always I had to explain *why* I wanted something, which translated into: "What did you do to deserve it?" and "You can't always have what you want." Simply saying "I want" was never quite good enough.

I lived in that lovely house like a lady in waiting until I left to find out what else I might be. Mom keeps my bedroom filled with fresh flowers, but until I know more about what I want for my own life, it doesn't make any sense to go home again.

—MARIA is a fashion model and graphic artist

Psychoanalysis still preserves the initiatory pattern. The patient is asked to descend deeply into himself, to make his past live, to confront his traumatic experiences again. . . . This dangerous operation resembles initiatory descents into hell, the realm of ghosts, and combats with monsters.
MIRCEA ELIADE,
The Sacred and the Profane

TRIBES

*I pledge allegiance to the
Flag of the United
States of America, and
to the Republic for
which it stands, One
Nation . . .*

Pre-modern peoples didn't think of themselves as individuals—they were members of a tribe as well as of a
family. Ancient philosophers knew that human dignity begins with "We are a people, therefore I am."
Modern people are tribal too but we call our tribes by
different names—churches, corporations, states, nations. Each of us was nurtured within and shaped by
several corporate bodies, voluntary organizations and
professional corporations that molded our values and
behavior—schools, athletic teams, businesses, clubs,
temples, and local, national, and international govern-
ments.

Viewpoints

Those organizations in which we learn and work
absorb the major part of the time we spend away from
families. Schools and businesses create an important
part of the mythology of our clan: "Education is the
key to success."

- Draw floor plans of your earliest schoolrooms.
  Which of Mrs. Brace's litanies still clutter your
  mind? ("Raise your hand before speaking." "Set the
  example, don't *be* the example.") How did you feel
  on the first and last days of school? What values did
  you learn along with arithmetic? (Citizenship?
  Good conduct? Respect for authority?)

And, "Financial success is the foundation of lasting
happiness."

- What did you first get paid to do?
- What part has work played in your life? Is it
  different from play? What do you value more? How
  valuable would you be without it?

We move in and out of groups and organizations.
Each corporate body has its way of defining member-

ship. Construct a collage from the symbols of your loyalties.

- What uniforms or emblems have you worn? (Scout? Marine? Nurse? Matron? Sex goddess? Motorcycle helmet?)
- What pledges have you taken, what creeds affirmed? (On my honor I will . . ." "I believe in . . .") How many do you still honor? Did you honor them at the time?
- What secret initiations have you undergone and what was your reward?

National allegiance is the modern equivalent of tribal loyalty. Patriotism is the magic of transferring familial feelings (Fatherland, Motherland) to a political entity. This trick is accomplished by creating a national history which all citizens share. The younger generation is initiated into the stories that the People (Zulus, Americans, Comanches, Cubans) have always told.

- What does it mean to you to have African, Polish, German, Mexican, Armenian blood?
- What are your distinguishing national characteristics? What stories and jokes taught you that the Irish brawl, Jews make money, French make love, Mexicans are lazy, Americans are foolish, and other stereotypes?

Bitterly Hoeing and Mowing

God knows how I loathe free time, so whenever He wants to punish me He makes me stop working. I manage to avoid manufactured three-day weekends and personal vacations, but legal holidays are inescapable. Even if I go to the office as usual there's no one around to hand me manuscripts or respond to my memos or bring me coffee. I usually end up going to some damn office party which only exacerbates my frustration.

To the ancient Greek the discovery of private identity was a terrifying and horrible thing that came about with the discovery of visual space and fragmentary classification. Twentieth-century man is traveling the reverse course, from an extreme individual fragmentary state back into a condition of corporate involvement with all mankind. Paradoxically, this new involvement is experienced as alienation and loss of private selfhood.
MARSHALL MCLUHAN
AND HARLEY PARKER

Modern totalitarianism in America works in subtle ways. It has no flag but the company logotype, and no weapons but paychecks, promotions, and the promise of happiness.
EARL SHORRIS

The corporation or the bureaucracy . . . becomes a place, the cultural authority, the moral home of a man. The rules of the corporation become the rules of society, the future replaces history, and the organization becomes the family. . . .
As the corporation separates men from each other, making a class of competing atoms, it gains control over them.
EARL SHORRIS

A good workday is something I can feel the instant I wake up in the morning. If I'm not abnormally depressed or hung over, my fingers and toes start wiggling and right away my head's popping with great ideas. During breakfast I chew on plans and memos and then rush to the office. On the best days everything goes smoothly into gear with me at the wheel.

I haven't always loved my work. As a kid I spent half my life bitterly hoeing and mowing. We had a hopeless lawn, cows, and no fence, and my mother had a way of making everything doubly unpleasant. It was a lousy lawn, a lousy house, a lousy life. Once I tried to throw over the whole thing, permanently. I got appendicitis and ate a box of epsom salts and spent my sixteenth birthday in the hospital trying to die.

My father was a skilled plumber and mechanic. I worked in his garage for twelve years. Then I went away to college and learned, in a freshman physics course, how a combustion engine is put together. My father knew a lot, but he never taught me any of it. He was such a good craftsman that he must have had some joy or pride in him, but even that he managed to keep hidden.

Before I became an editor I was a reporter for a large newspaper. I didn't have any of the money or status or authority that I have now, but I felt self-righteous just the same because I was working so hard. Newspaper work meant daily pressure and steady teamwork. I loved the intensity. I think it was during those years that I established myself as out of sync with mankind: I had Wednesdays and Thursdays off, so I escaped those horrid weekends that drove other people into society.

If I were suddenly forced to retire, I'd probably kill myself. When I'm working I'm potent and important. It's not the same anyplace else in my life. I often envy my kids because they don't work and don't seem to need to, but I'm too far gone for that. Besides, there's always the danger that if I stopped driving myself I'd find how nice it feels and never work again. . . . I'd end up running off to Acapulco and receding into lower-middle-class penury, and then God would spite me and I'd be mowing lawns again!

A life of leisure is out of the question. I only know how to relax under the pressure and concentration of hard work. When I lose myself in problem-solving I feel (for a short time) powerful and collected. As long as the world's workload holds out, I'm sure I'll go on working like a maniac, placating God, and resenting my children. After all, I do all that so terribly well. . . .

—ROBERT is a middle-aged newspaper editor
with a passion for exactness

Walking to Work

I figure that a person's work is whatever he does best. For me, that's walking. Twenty-two years ago, when I was forty, I dropped out and slowed down and never checked in again. I live off a small veteran's pension. Every morning I wake up early, walk down the hill to town, and start strolling. I look at things and think about things and say hello and good-bye to whomever I happen to pass. Sometimes I go to the post office to check my box and stare at the mail, or to the bakery for a cup of coffee. Often I sit for several hours on the bus bench, watching traffic and feeling the sun on me. In between I just walk.

It took me years to learn how to do this well. At first I was always interrupting myself, asking guilty questions like: What are you producing? What do you do for other people? One thing I'm sure of, I'm not doing anyone any harm. Most people spend their days making cookies and doorknobs and weapons. I feel my body swinging down the street and know I'm doing at least as much as those people do. Anyway, with over half the output in America wasted on war and defense, I'm glad to be a noncontributor. . . .

So my job is walking down the street celebrating the existence of things. Someone's got to do it! This is a small town and a lot of people probably think I'm crazy—Harvard graduate wandering around like the town bum for twenty years—but I don't care. I'm too busy appreciating the clouds and trees and sounds that most people rush right past. These things need to be celebrated, so how can I stop to worry about what I'm *not* doing?

Every night when I go to sleep I die, and every morning

I been working on the railroad, all the live-long day,
I been working on the railroad just to pass the time away
Don't you hear the whistle blowin'? Rise up so early in the morn
Don't you hear the Cap'n shoutin', Dinah, blow your horn?
North American railroad work song

I'm born again. I walk and see and "emanate"—as Robert Graves would say. All the time I'm thinking and watching myself grow fuller and lighter over the years. It's a fine life's work; I'm good at it, and there's no retirement in sight.

—VINCENT is a sixty-two-year-old
bachelor and iconoclast

THE GEOGRAPHY OF THE PSYCHE

The seat of the soul is where the inner world and the outer world meet. Where they overlap, it is in every point of the overlap.
NOVALIS

We can't separate who we are from where we are. People are rooted in time and place, so our psychic space is generously seasoned with memories of physical territories. The Montana-born may feel claustrophobic in city streets that seem spacious to New Yorkers. The geography of our past is part of memory.

The link between turf and psyche is the result of early associations. When you were a child there probably were places you could and couldn't go. We learned to connect busy streets and the yards of cranky neighbors with the dangerous unknown. Later the same taboos were extended to tattoo parlors, whorehouses, and neighborhoods on the other side of the tracks. Every human emotion is seeded in the sights, smells, sounds, and tastes of specific environments.

It is possible to explore the geography of your psyche by reconstructing the places where you have lived. Start with the smell of a pizza parlor and it might lead you back to your first date. Conversely, emotions can be traced backward to specific places: panic may be connected with the image of being smothered under blankets or being lost in the woods; happiness may be a milk shake at the corner drugstore; freedom may be jetting through the night in the back seat of a 1956 Ford.

Viewpoints

Re-create with words or drawings the childhood environment you remember best. Concentrate on the

city or countryside that lay beyond the intimate space
you occupied with your family.

- Take an imaginary walk through your home town
  and see what people, places, smells, and feelings pop
  up.
- What places were taboo? Where *didn't* you go?
- What social, regional, political, class, and economic
  peculiarities of your environment seasoned your
  early life?
- What aspects of your early locales are still real and
  important to you? Which have you moved away
  from?

The Fishnet

When we moved to Southern California from the East
Coast I was deeply impressed by four things: the wide, sandy
beaches; the mass of cars (especially forest-green Porsches)
on the road; people walking around half-naked; and the
bold pink paint job on my grammar school.

Our town was a neat middle-class suburb of Los Angeles,
caught up on three sides by multi-lane freeways and major
boulevards, circled by Hollywood and Beverly Hills, Culver
City used-car lots, huge aeronautics plants, the International
Airport, and the dusty old downtown area a dozen miles
east. During my twelve years there I remember exactly two
family trips downtown: one to see *Flower Drum Song* at the
Shrine Auditorium and the other to order a pair of glasses
from the City Teachers' Optical Exchange. The town was
like a fish tangled in a huge net. Those of us who lived north
of the tracks coped with the existence of Los Angeles largely
by ignoring it. We kept to ourselves, clinging to the sleek
public beaches on our western border.

Every sunny summer day we went to the beach and swam
and played volleyball and laid around on beach towels with
Cokes and candy bars and transistor radios. A couple of miles
south of lifeguard stand number 2, where our crowd

Country Roads, take me home,
To the place I belong,
West Virginia, mountain momma,
Take me home, Country Roads.
BILL DANOFF, TAFFY NIVERT, AND JOHN DENVER,
"Take Me Home, Country Roads"

*Since religious man can-
not live except in an at-
mosphere impregnated
with the sacred, we must
expect to find a large
number of techniques for
consecrating space.*
MIRCEA ELIADE,
The Sacred and the Profane

*A Navaho hogan is . . .
constructed of logs and
adobe, always with eight
sides and with its one
door opening east to the
sunrise. The smoke-
opening in the domed
roof corresponds to the
mythological opening in
the heaven dome. The
fireplace in the center of
the floor is symbolically
the center of the world.*
JOSEPH CAMPBELL,
*The Way of the Animal
Powers*

gathered, was an old fishing pier that reeked of bait and fried fish and cotton candy. The clientele was mostly senior citizens and Muscle Beach bodybuilders, so anytime we got bored we walked down there for a free show. In the late afternoons we straggled home with the soles of our feet burned from asphalt and hot sand, and smelling of salt water and Coppertone. My girlfriends and I stripped naked in front of the bathroom mirror and compared our young bodies, all of them smooth and brown and blond.

The endless summers faded by late October. Winter days were moderately cool with occasional rain or fog. I loved to see the palm trees with their tops lopped off by sheets of fog, and to smell the air stained with eucalyptus after a good rain. But I didn't really pay much attention to trees. By the time I was in high school the slick, bleached, one-dimensional Southern California style seemed 100 percent normal to me. The laundromat, bowling alley, bakery dispensary, cycle shop, crabgrass lawns, and taco stand dripping with ground beef that I passed on my way to school were the other half of the world to me. High school was made up of oatmeal cookies, eraser crumbs, bus fumes, and dirty gym clothes. What else was there?

It was only when I left town after graduation that I saw what my town didn't have. Other parts of the country had different attractions: winter, spring, and fall; clear air; street theater and town meetings; farms and vegetable gardens; psychic healing and new music. I saw how life in suburban Los Angeles had flattened me. I'd learned to be cool and flowing, but not to stand out or think creatively or go for broke.

So for a long time I was fascinated with anything ethnic or eccentric. At nineteen I remember listening to a Russian/Jewish–American poet read her poems with such vigorous feeling that I sat in the audience and wept over my own lack of "heritage" or "character," resolving to flee to Georgia or southern France where I'd grow pecans or learn a language with soul!

Instead I went to San Francisco, Manhattan, Montana, and Washington, D.C., and even back to Los Angeles for awhile to live downtown with "the people." Now I'm ready to settle somewhere, but the question is, where? I like fluidity and expanse (as in freeways and ocean) but I hate the predictable, monoemotional nature of what I grew up in. I need color and sharp edges as well as roots. I need to belong to something I make for myself. But where is it? And what is it? A place? A work? A people? I've dropped pieces of myself all over the place, and now I want to gather some of them together.

—ANNE is a woman in her mid-twenties,
constantly on the move

The Wilderness Within

Beneath my urban exterior there are pine trees, sage grass, and redheaded woodpeckers.

I had an old-fashioned childhood, much more like Tom Sawyer's than Holden Caulfield's. My family moved every year or two from one small southern town to another. This meant that my brother and I were always outsiders, handy scapegoats for the established gangs. In rubber-gun and BB-gun wars we were the targets. But the moment we took to the woods we were foxes. We ran along invisible paths and lost our pursuers with ease and then circled around to laugh at their confusion. No one could trace us to our hidden lairs. I remember one fortress we made beneath a large fallen tree. We hollowed out a space and wove saplings together to form the sides and top and camouflaged the whole thing with fallen branches. It was so well hidden that it took us several tries before we could find it on the run. Occasionally some earnest scoutmaster would bring a troop of forty boys into our woods for tests in tracking and woodmanship. On those glorious days we changed trail markers, laid false trails, and stalked around creating unbelievable chaos. To this day I have dreams in which someone is chasing me in the woods, but for me these are delightful. I know I can pull out a trick or two and outwit my pursuers.

No matter where I am in the world I can feel the mud from the creek ooze up between my toes and the cool water from the swimming hole dripping off my body when I need to. My images of absolute harmony are of lying in the grass in the sun getting dry and warm and listening to the

According to the traditions of the Achilpa tribe, the divine being Numbakula fashioned a sacred pole from the trunk of a gum tree, and after anointing it with blood, climbed it and disappeared into the sky. This pole represents the cosmic axis, for it is around the sacred pole that territory becomes habitable. . . . During their wanderings the Achilpa always carry the pole with them. . . . This allows them, while being continually on the move, to be always in "their world" and, at the same time, in communication with the sky into which Numbakula vanished.
MIRCEA ELIADE,
The Sacred and the Profane

gurgling of the water, and of walking home in the dusk when a silver note of a wood thrush rises up to join the light of the first star. At the end of the day we were happy to be going home to a warm dinner and parents who were just as glad to see us returning as they had been to get rid of us that morning.

—SANDOR is a gentleman farmer, husband, and father

Words Never Worked

The world of today is sick to its thin blood for lack of elemental things, for fire before the hands, for water welling from the earth, for air, for the dear earth underfoot. In my world of beach and dune these elemental presences lived and had their being. . . . The flux and reflux of ocean, the incoming of waves, the gatherings of birds . . . winter and storm—all these were part of the great beach.
HENRY BESTON,
The Outermost House

The eight of us—plus poor old Elizabeth McCarthy before she dropped dead in the attic room—lived in a huge beat-up asbestos house in small-town Massachusetts. The place was a wreck. Paint-chipped walls, stains, knobs missing from doors, and that damp back room with the hanging light bulb where we buried the winter's rubbers and ice skates and sweaters—all reeking with mold. There were two garbage cans in the front yard that marked our compound. They were crawling with maggots. Even now it gives me the creeps to think of my mother's hands inspecting us for worms.

It wasn't that we were destitute so much as that no one much cared about keeping things together. Father worked all day in a dye factory and couldn't cope very well when he came home. He would wander around the house babbling in incoherent Italian/New England/alcoholese. Mother nursed at the mental hospital every night till midnight. The rest of the family watched a lot of TV, generally avoiding one another.

Our gangly household was centered around one basic taboo: no real conversation allowed. In a thousand unspoken ways we were discouraged from saying anything substantial to one another. Father waited up every night for Mother to come home (he's probably there now, snoring in the maroon chair, insulated by the TV) and as soon as she was in the door they started up their noisy battles. Over and over they shouted the same accusations, but since neither one ever listened you couldn't really call it communication. Occasionally one of them would slobber out an "I love you" or something to one of us, but that didn't mean much either. Outside of our parents' cyclical hostilities there was just no room in our house for emotional expressions.

There were, however, occasional moratoriums, days when the cold war was dropped and we all talked and touched each other. Christmas, Easter, and Thanksgiving were like bright slides flashed on a blank screen. The constricting taboos were set aside and we were generous and affectionate, even excessive (having saved up all year!) with one another. All of a sudden the eight of us shared a unified dream, even if it was only a belief in Santa Claus. It was fabulous. I remember how one Christmas Eve the priest announced that God was real but Santa wasn't. On the way home from mass Mom and Dad told us not to worry about it, that this time the Father was mistaken, and we gladly believed them. Holidays were rare occasions for me, times when I didn't have to worry about my tender feelings hanging out.

Two years ago Mother insisted, as she always does, that everyone come home for Thanksgiving dinner. I knew it was impossible, but for the hundredth time the desire to be at ease, to be part of a family that *talked* to one another got the best of me. We assembled, thirteen of us now, dead-ended around the living room, wondering what to say to one another, fighting the urge to switch on the television. Mother was in the kitchen completing the last details of dinner. Finally she brought it all out—turkey, cranberries, peas, onions, mashed potatoes, sweet potatoes, pickles, jellies, bread, pies, strong Irish coffee—and placed it, chilled and steaming, on the long table while the rest of us watched.

After she lifted her fork Mother excused herself, went upstairs, overdosed herself with barbiturates, and passed out. I found her draped on the bed and called an ambulance. At the hospital they pumped her stomach and tucked her in to sleep it off. Mother hadn't intended to die. She told me later she saw Father kissing a neighbor over the back fence and "just had to do something to change the rules." Words had never worked with them, so she gathered her most vulnerable audience and staged a statement of her anger, one which we all understood.

After the hospital phoned to say that Mother would be all

In the woods one of the satisfactions is to return to places that are associated with events in my life, that I am bound to by more than familarity and affection; places I hunted or wandered in when I was a boy, where I have walked and picnicked with Tanya and the children and with friends, where ideas and words have come to me. . . . Tanya says one reason we are happy here is that we are learning where to expect things to happen.
WENDELL BERRY,
A Continuous Harmony

right, the rest of us crept to the table and picked away at the
cold feast in silence.

—JEAN is a modern dancer and choreographer
from an Italian New England family

MORALS, MANNERS, AND FOLK TALES

Culture is a machine for conserving, discovering, and
sharing knowledge. Knowledge is conveyed by two
processes: teaching and learning.

Teaching requires a formal situation in which there
is a clear distinction between the informed and the
ignorant. Before we are old enough to defend ourselves, parents, preachers, teachers, and advertisers
systematically teach us the myths, morals, and manners
they believe we need to know in order to be civilized.
But learning often takes place unconsciously and
informally. Usually we learn best when we are enjoying ourselves most: songs, jokes, and stories told just
for the fun of it worm their way into our imaginations
and nibble at the core of our more serious beliefs.

The things we learn by ourselves—the knowledge
we assimilated by osmosis when Dylan sang, "The
times they are a-changing"—strike deeper than the
lessons that were formally taught to us. We were
taught that all people are equal in the eyes of God and
the law, but in stereotyped stories and jokes we
gathered that "Polocks," "niggers," "queers," spin-
sters, "retards," and stutterers were not quite right and
not equal. We were taught that honesty is the best
policy, but we saw that actually tact (lying), cleverness
(cheating), and legal loopholes (stealing) were accepta-
ble aids for getting along in the world. Official morals
and myths are ideals, not actualities, and no culture
wholly believes in its own propaganda. Thus, what we
are taught comes to us tinged with conflict and
ambivalence, and that's really the way we pass it on.

Viewpoints

Some of the tension and ambiguity you experienced within yourself may be a result of contradictory messages received as a child from parents and other adults. Because their ideals and their actualities were at war with each other, they may have said one thing and done another. They had enough cynicism and idealism to warn you: "Do as I say, not as I do," but while they instructed you in their hopes, their fears came alive for you too.

- What ten commandments would best summarize the rules, ideals, and taboos your family advocated? (You shall earn your living and your dignity by work. You shall appear moderate, polite, and gentle no matter how you feel.)
- What jokes, stories, clichés, and slogans were told until they were as polished as riverbed pebbles? What were the unconscious messages hidden within your family's oral tradition?
- What feelings about sex did you get from "dirty" jokes and formal sex instruction?
- Who were the good and bad, clean and dirty characters in your family lore? What jokes were told?

The Texas Ranger

When I was a boy Dad told me a story I never forgot. In the early forties, driving through Texas, he stopped at a diner where an old-timer asked him if he was driving toward Dallas. Dad said yes and invited the stranger to ride along. As they drove through the long night the man began to tell stories about his days as a Texas Ranger. He told about the time he and another ranger thought they had a killer trapped in a cabin. They called for him to come out and were answered by gunfire. They shot back. When the battle was over there were three dead men in the cabin, but it turned out that none of them was the suspect. As the

The Army. Be all that you can be. The greatest challenge of them all. Yourself.

stranger got out of the car in Dallas he said to my father, "I've seen a lot of things I wish I hadn't seen."

I think Dad told me this story as a kind of warning: watch what you do because the consequences of a false move will scar you for life. For years I respected this message. I was afraid of making irreparable mistakes because I didn't know about second and third chances. But finally I broke some rules and took some risks and buried my father, and the whole thing turned over. Now I think that what I'll regret most when I'm old is not anything I've seen or done but the things I was simply too timid to try.

—Roy is a teacher and storyteller

Relics And Talismans

There are things that promise to outlast all of us. Bach is dead and his music is everywhere. One way mortals defy time is by investing themselves in durable things that can be passed from generation to generation. Such inherited objects are a mixed blessing. While we gain power from inheritance we are also defined and limited by it: we come trailing streams of karma and leading white elephants.

The things that one generation wills to another insure continuity. Cultures differ in their ideas of what possessions, rights, and obligations of the fathers should be visited upon the children. It may be land, titles, livestock, wives, ceremonial equipment and religious rites, songs, personal clothing and body adornments, antiques, money, stocks and bonds. All souvenirs are reminders of what has come before us. Part of each person's life is recorded in the objects he leaves to his survivors.

Viewpoints

Legacies come in tangible and intangible forms.

- **What heirlooms have you inherited? (Antiques? Jewelry? Clothing? Books? Property?)**

- What objects of sentimental or personal significance do you have that once belonged to someone else? (Conjuring stones? A wedding ring? Lock of hair? Pictures?) Why do you keep them?
- To what extent has inherited money shaped your life?
- What personal qualities were gifts from persons who are no longer living? Whom are you living up to? Who died for you?

Thinking about the residue that will remain after you die is a good way to clarify the values in which you are now investing your time and energy.

- Make an imaginary will in which you bequeath your personal and financial possessions. Note which things you value most.
- What personal qualities would you like to assign to family and friends? Which do you hope to bury with you?

so much depends upon

a red wheel barrow

glazed with rain water

beside the white chickens
WILLIAM CARLOS WILLIAMS,
from *Spring and All*

Driftwood and Love Letters

When Dad died my relic stock pile instantly doubled. He owned little of economic value, few antiques, no land or money. The things he loved were all sensory objects: Navajo rugs, a turquoise belt buckle, a seventy-pound shell of a man-eating clam, pieces of driftwood he found and fondled, little medicine bottles full of polished stones or sea shells or copper pennies, and an old hickory walking stick with a fistlike gnarl at one end which he rubbed with oil and crushed wheat until it was perfectly cured. I chose these things to keep because they remind me of the special way my father had of touching things, of using his hands to relate to the world. From him I inherited a kind of permission to caress what is beautiful.

My mother and grandmother used to sew clothes for me. When I was thirteen they made me a brown cowboy shirt

The fetish object . . . is a supercharged locus of meaning, self-designated as of supreme importance for potential satisfaction. . . . The question that arises is this: How far can one narrow down his grip on the world, and still be in it in "human" fashion? The fetishist is said to be near to psychosis precisely because his wedge into the object world is so narrow.
ERNEST BECKER,
Angels in Armor

embroidered in beautiful greens and oranges. When I moved from Tennessee to Delaware the kids teased me for looking like Tex Ritter, so I hung the shirt up. But I've kept it all these years because my dreams of woods and animals and wide-open spaces are woven into it.

I keep my personal memorabilia in an artillery-shell trunk in a closet. It contains old diaries, newspaper clippings, snapshots, souvenirs from my trip out West at seventeen, my Eagle Scout badge, and love letters from all my old girl friends. There are also letters from my fifth-grade teacher, Miss Beech, who drew birds in pastels on the stationery and wrote that I was "tough as a tiger." I don't want all of this stuff directly around me, but I don't want to throw it away either. It's a way of preserving my past without actually having to lug it with me. The photographs are especially good that way. They whisper, *"You were there,"* about stages along my way, reminding me that I came from somewhere.

—ROY

The Glass Box

These I have loved: White plates and cups, clean-gleaming, ringed with blue lines; . . . wet roofs, beneath the lamplight; the strong crust of friendly bread; . . . the rough male kiss of blankets; grainy wood; live hair that is shining and free; blue-massing clouds; the keen unpassioned beauty of a great machine; the benison of hot water; furs to touch; the good smell of old clothes . . .
RUPERT BROOKE

My grandfather was a turn-of-the-century robber baron, a giant who took what he wanted. Anyone who owned an oil field within his reach had reason to worry. Grandfather came on like a tidal wave, crushing and liquidating everything in his path. He was a classic Oil King. My father inherited a fortune and at the age of thirty decided to sit it out: no work, no society, no real friends. Now he and my mother dole out huge hunks of money to me, like monthly dog biscuits. I guess that arrangement makes me *dependently* wealthy, but anyway I'm very rich. . . .

I was born in a gilded crib that was heavy as gold. For forty-one years I've been languishing in it like Scrooge in his money bins, and it's not likely to dry up. I'm attached to the things money buys. My clothes are simple but obviously expensive and tasteful; they make me a country gentleman. I love fast cars and schooners, and the power to arrive anywhere, anytime. My money buys superior education and homes for me and my family. It also insures that we will never starve or go unattended. Grandfather's fortune sets me apart from other people.

But money inhibits too. At five I was the perfect little gentleman, perfectly polite, superior and stifled. My mother made a habit of pointing her finger at people who made fools of themselves, teaching me by negative example to avoid extremes. I was courteous, thoughtful, obedient, well mannered, and completely sheltered from all expressions of anger or ecstasy. Women without breeding were known to be lurking everywhere, hoping to cast a spell over me and my money.

So I lived like a rare orchid painted into a landscape, so protected from the hard, real-world experiences which define most people that I grew up smooth, without muscles or scars. While the other kids were out tearing around town on their paper routes, I was in my glass box keeping clean. I remember the time my father gave me a Brownie box camera. I liked it a lot, so right away he bought me an expensive Leica, which killed the excitement. I felt overwhelmed and left out.

The real things I needed from my father he never offered. His single message about sex, for instance, was that if he ever caught me carrying contraceptives (and he would find out, he said, because they leave rings on wallet leather) he'd beat the hell out of me. I was fifteen, and that was the first and last word from him, but somehow I inherited his sexual timidities.

So I floated through college and the Army looking out of my glass box, but nothing got through to me. I took on some wives and children and hobbies but still avoided the world, living inside my own loneliness. I began to see myself as a pool of gelatin—not Jello, which has a flavor— but an inert blob that does nothing.

I was so submerged in my legacy that up until a couple of years ago I had no idea what I desired. Finally, greatly depressed, I deduced that the elegant, timeless existence that money provides is not enough, that a person needs a work, a skill. I went back to school to earn a degree in filmmaking.

My wife says that my "menopausal ambitions" to become a film maker are unrealistic. I'm banking on the hope that

The mysterious woman took from the bundle a pipe. . . . Holding the pipe up with its stem to the heavens, she said: "With this sacred pipe you will walk upon the Earth; for the Earth is your Grandmother and Mother, and She is sacred. Every step that is taken upon Her should be a prayer. The bowl of the pipe is red stone; it is the Earth. Carved in the stone and facing the center is this buffalo calf, who represents all the four-leggeds who live upon your Mother. The stem of the pipe is of wood, and this represents all that grows upon the Earth."
BLACK ELK

she's wrong. Reaching out like this is very painful, but by now it's do or die. I get terribly limp and despondent sometimes, but even in my worst depressions I never consider renouncing my fortune. It's too late for that. The prestige and security of having money holds me together like a cellophane skin. Even professional competency isn't likely to relieve that dependency, but I still have hopes of being acknowledged and useful to society, of pulling myself up from the gilded bed. I don't want to die of the old family disease. . . .

—SHELDON is a middle-aged man who lives in a mansion
overlooking the Pacific Ocean

GIFTS AND WOUNDS

Everyone alive has received some share of the gifts that make and keep human life human. The giving and receiving of gifts plays a large part in most cultures. Gift giving is rooted in the primal feeling that the world itself is a gift, a banquet already spread before us when we arrive on the scene. Something—chance, God, the trickster, or divine reason—arranged things to support human life. The rains come, the corn grows, and the yearly harvest is followed by a thanksgiving festival. We give gifts because life is given to us. We can repress it or throw it away, but we can't hold onto it. Psychological research suggests that people most predisposed to develop cancer are those who fail to express their emotions. Generosity is a recycling of the gifts of life.

Wounds are as universal as gifts: sooner or later suffering and death strike us all. The ancients wove myths around this basic ambiguity of life. Father Time (the Greek god Chronos) is the devourer of his children; Kali (the Hindu goddess of creativity) often appears with motherly arms and blood dripping from her lips.

In a famous case in American law Justice Holmes decided the suit of a blind man against a construction company for injuries received when the man fell into

If it had not been for this thing, I might have lived out my life talking at street corners to scorning men. I might have died unmarked, unknown, a failure. Now we are not a failure. This is our career and our triumph. Never in our full life could we hope to do such work for tolerance, for justice, for man's understanding of man, as now we do by accident. . . . Our words, our lives—our pains: nothing. The taking of our lives— lives of a good shoemaker and a poor fish peddler—all! That last moment belongs to us— that agony is our triumph.
BARTOLOMEO VANZETTI, letter to his son before Vanzetti's execution

an open ditch. The ditch had been marked with smudge pots and signs but the blind man, who refused to use a cane or any other device to guide him, missed the warnings. Holmes argued that, since society is composed of persons who are all crippled and limited in some way, each person has the obligation to protect others from his own limitations. The blind man forfeited his right to damages when he transferred to others the responsibility for dealing with his affliction. Society is a brotherhood of the gifted and the wounded. As individuals we differ only in the composition of our assets and limitations.

That society is unjust often means that one man's gift is another man's wound. Scarsdale and Harlem, wealth and poverty, privilege and oppression coexist in unholy symbiosis. But things are more than what they seem. Rich is better than hungry, but injustice may create a supportive community among victims while the exploiters suffer anomie. Anxiety and madness can be the price of creative genius. Gifts and wounds fit together like yang and yin.

Viewpoints

Resentment, anger, and hostility are gauges of the real and imaginary injuries you have suffered.

- What persons, events, and institutions arouse your greatest resentment or anger? Who frustrated, neglected, manipulated, inhibited, or repressed you?
- In what ways have wounds made you stronger?

Gratitude is the expected response to a gift. But gifts may also trigger feelings of embarrassment, obligation, or confusion.

- What gifts have bound you to the giver, made you dependent, weaker? Did you realize it at the time, or only later?
- When have you been singled out for special atten-

Grace strikes us when we are in great pain and restlessness. . . . It strikes us when our disgust for our own being, our weakness, our hostility, and our lack of direction and composure have become intolerable to us. It strikes us when, year after year, the longed-for perfection of life does not appear, when the old compulsions reign with us as they have for decades . . . Sometimes at that moment a wave of light breaks into our darkness, and it is as though a voice were saying: "You are accepted. . . ."
PAUL TILLICH,
The Shaking of the Foundations

tion? What persons have enriched your life by caring, teaching, challenging, delighting in you?

- Flip your story. Make a convincing argument that your gifts are wounds and limitations and that what you previously considered wounds or causes for resentment are actually blessings. (Does your beauty isolate you even while it attracts?)

The Sins of the Fathers

Above all we need to be taught more affection for the infirmities of life. . . . Both artist and lover know that perfection is not lovable. It is the clumsiness of a fault that makes a person lovable. . . . This is a common theme in the folklore of Arabian Nights: *where you stumble and fall, there you find the gold.*
JOSEPH CAMPBELL, conversation with Sam Keen, *Psychology Today*

Life is either an adventure, or it is nothing.
HELEN KELLER

When I was seven, my parents wrote a letter to the archbishop of Virginia complaining that one of his schools would not accept their good Catholic daughter. The archbishop finally arranged for my admission, but that was no blessing for me. The kids whispered "nigger" and the teachers gave me low grades, assuming, I guess, that black skin comes thick. I wasn't brought up to hate whites and didn't understand all this. My father was a noncommissioned Army officer. He and my mother wanted money, nice cars, 2.5 college-educated kids, and a home of their own just like everyone else.

I clung to the idea that someone was going to help me get what I needed until the day I got my ass up to college and found myself tromping through the snow with borrowed books and no coat, freezing to death. I had to rethink things. I was in college to please my parents, but they weren't paying anything; I was tied to a series of scholarships; I was bored and uneasy. Suddenly I had no idea why I was doing any of it.

When I read W. E. B. Du Bois and Malcolm X and Eldridge Cleaver for the first time, I started changing. I no longer wanted to accumulate things the way my parents did—just to show the neighbors they could do it. I joined the Black Student Union and for a while my hope was in pure Black Power, but when I found out that the Union was funded and controlled by whites and that our president kept a white girl on the side, I faded out. I stopped thinking *help your brothers* and started thinking *help yourself.* Racism was already institutionalized, Molotov cocktails or Civil Rights Amendments wouldn't change anything. I dropped out of school and got a secretarial job in another town.

I'm only twenty, but being black in America has already taught me to be a good jungle animal. I'm clever and flexible; I know how to change colors to get through hard situations. One day I walked into a drugstore and a wrinkled old lady looked at my afro and she says, "Why do you wear your hair like that? I think it's *disgusting!*" I had a dozen ways to respond. I could have mouthed her back, or ignored her, or mocked her by Uncle Tom-ing, but this old bitch was so dilapidated that I felt sorry for her. I looked straight into her scabby old eyes for a few seconds and walked out.

Being black in a white land means you've got to care a lot about yourself in order to survive. You either learn to stay on your toes or you get trampled. Every day I have to fight the stereotypes they lay on me, otherwise someday when I'm discouraged and someone suggests that my skin makes me dirty or stupid or lazy I might start believing it. Stereotypes are deadly for anyone. Counteracting mine keeps me flexible.

I don't believe in revenge, but I'm not going to help Whitey clean up his messes either. The Mafia shot heroin into the black ghettos and whites watched addicts flying off rooftops and said, "Good. That makes one less nigger!" But when white GIs started getting wired, the big men suddenly decided they had a drug problem! As far as I'm concerned, it would do them all good to walk around stoned for a while. . . . The reason I don't go in for revenge is that I know we all get paid back anyhow. There's a passage in the Bible that says, "The sins of the fathers are visited on the children," and I believe it. Maybe you don't pay immediately like George Wallace did, but sooner or later the chickens come to roost. We've all got relatives, and they all made stupid mistakes.

Sometimes I wish I could be loose and cool and let it all hang out like other kids these days. I'm so damn rational and serious, but how can I afford not to be? I know that whatever I want done for myself, I've got to do. Later on I'll have time to luxuriate and count the times people put me down but now I'm working toward a time when people who want to live and let live can get together, clean out

Stare deep into the world before you as if it were the void: innumerable holy ghosts, bhuddies and savior gods there hide, smiling. All the atoms emitting light inside wavehood, there is no personal separation of any of it. A hummingbird can come into a house and a hawk will not: so rest and be assured. While looking for the light, you may suddenly be devoured by the darkness and find the true light.
JACK KEROUAC

Only the wounded healer heals.
T. S. ELIOT

those who don't, and get down to it. And that revolution won't be all black. Look at me, my grandmother was Indian and my mother's family immigrated from the Caribbean someplace, so I don't even know where my color comes from! The truth is that no amount of money or tears can make up for the past, so why not let it go? Me, I'm getting ready for the good times!

—LEA has decided to go to law school

HEROES AND VILLAINS

The hero must venture forth from the world of commonsense consciousness into a region of supernatural wonder.
There he encounters fabulous forces—demons and angels, dragons and helping spirits. After a fierce battle, he wins a decisive victory over the powers of darkness.
Then he returns from his mysterious adventure with the gift of knowledge or fire, which he bestows on his fellow man.
JOSEPH CAMPBELL, conversation with Sam Keen, *Psychology Today*

There are always good guys and bad guys. Stories and personalities would be dull without them. In myths the good guys are very good and the bad ones are dark (and interesting) as sin. It helps to exaggerate good and evil and to create clear targets because in real life the best and the worst are so entwined that we usually can't tell which is which. Dr. Jekyll and Mr. Hyde are in fact united. Exaggeration pulls apart what life joins together; because life is complex we invent heroes and heroines. We learn from churches, schools, TV sitcoms, melodramas, and the silver screen how to tell the white hats from the black hats; they instruct us as assiduously as any primitive mythology ever taught its adherents to locate the friends and enemies of God.

Viewpoints

Trace the history of the heroes and heroines you have admired and imitated as personality models. Begin with your earliest heroes and bring the tale up to the present. Whom did you admire when you were five, fifteen, twenty-one? Distinguish between official and unofficial heroes (your parents may have been pleading the cause of St. Francis while you were secretly working with Captain America).

- What heroes and heroines did you find in books? In the movies? On TV? In real life?

- What costumes did you wear?
- Whose speech did you imitate?
- If your heroes and heroines could speak to you now, what advice would they give?
- What figures were held up to you as horrible villains?
- What public personalities, movie stars, politicians, sports heroes, and so on, do you emulate in your dress, speech, grooming?
- Have any of your heroes and villains switched places over the years? Why?

Heroes Don't Wear Glasses

My earliest heroes were all military figures in the traditional Nordic mold. A hero was any person who received a mortal wound and was subsequently borne away to Valhalla in the arms of a statuesque blonde goddess or a government public relations secretary. I memorized stories about Congressional Medal of Honor winners, and for years was the star of show-and-tell sessions. I nearly got to skip a grade when I defined "posthumous" for my second-grade teacher.

When I realized that heroism was a dying business I looked around for a living hero. For a couple of years I was thoroughly enchanted by the exploits of John Glenn, who later became an astronaut. I realize that millions of kids thought of Glenn as a hero, but I knew who he was in the late fifties when he appeared on *Name That Tune* with Eddie Hodges, who later made a movie with Frank Sinatra about rubber trees. Glenn had just broken the transcontinental air-speed record in a Crusader Jet.

So by the time I entered second grade I had my whole life planned. I was going to be a test pilot and, if a war came along, an ace. My fame was secure. Then one day my mother took me to an optometrist. I sat in a dark room for a couple of hours and came home with a prescription for glasses, and it was not unlike a death in the family. Everyone knew the rules—you couldn't fly with glasses.

I can't say that I endured this mortal wound with any

The ancient masters were subtle, mysterious, profound, responsive. The depth of their knowledge is unfathomable. Because it is unfathomable, all we can do is describe their appearance. Watchful, like men crossing a winter stream. Alert, like men aware of danger. Courteous, like visiting guests. Yielding, like ice about to melt. Simple, like uncarved blocks of wood. Hollow, like caves. Opaque, like muddy water.
LAO TSU,
Tao Te Ching

The truth about the need for heroes is not easy for anyone to admit. . . . To become conscious of what one is doing to earn his feeling of heroism is the main self-analytic problem of life. Everything painful and sobering in what psychoanalytic genius and religious genius have discovered about man revolves around the terror of admitting what one is doing to earn his self-esteem.
ERNEST BECKER,
The Denial of Death

kind of nobility or grace. The day I got my glasses I sat in the parking lot searching for villains. I was past the age where I could blame the optometrist; I had betrayed myself. I sat there staring at a tree, seeing the individual leaves for the first time in my life. I thought about a heroic bomber pilot who, when he was shot down over the Pacific, ordered his crew to bail out and then flew his plane into the side of a Japanese battleship. I sat there looking at the tree, frustrated because I couldn't dive into what I saw. Clarity was my enemy.

I think this experience defined villainy for me. A villain was any person or event that prevented my dreams and wishes from coming true.

My next set of heroes came from television. Walt Disney had two western series featuring Texas John Slaughter and El Fego Baca. Texas John wore white and married an innocent schoolmarm. He was good but not all that bright, depending on luck and the bias of his script writers to defeat evil. Baca was a shadowy, Zorro-type figure with nine lives. He was competent and willing to risk his life every other week. (In fact, half the fascination was seeing how he would live up to his own legend!) Of the two, Baca had the most effect on me, although I have to admit that part of me would like to flash around in white as an impersonal agent of good. I guess I ended up incorporating both—light and dark, honesty and cunning.

My last hero came from literature, the wizard Gandalf in Tolkien's *Lord of the Rings.* He gave me the idea that the hero goes through stages and that most magic takes place within the self. Gandalf is an intermediary between the world and the watchers. As Gandalf the Grey he fights his demon, dies, and is returned as Gandalf the White. By dying he makes connection with the watchers. That happens to me sometimes. Something dies and I confront the part of me that watches, the detached observer, the little boy looking at leaves. When I emerge I am better.

My personified villains are harder for me to remember. The television variety always disappeared after one show, dead or run out of town. I do remember once volunteering to go to hell and assassinate the Devil. When the minister turned down my proposal I realized that Sunday school wasn't telling the real story. A Christian credibility gap. If there wasn't a villain, then the battle between good and evil wasn't all it was cracked up to be.

In junior high school I had regular fights with most of the juvenile delinquents in town, but I didn't take these personally—we were representatives of two permanently opposed forces. I was small, they were large; I was an egghead, they were tough, and we played our roles accordingly.

Gradually I'm learning that my worst enemies and best heroes are all within me. Whenever I try to shove that responsibility off on someone else, I get cut off from new possibilities. I'm like a citizen under old Chinese law who knows that if he kills a man he is responsible for the welfare of that man's family ever after. The burden of good and evil is mine. Knowing that, I do less worshiping these days. And if I met the Devil I'd probably apologize for listening to his detractors!

—JIM PETERSEN is the *Playboy* adviser

THE BELOVED ENEMY

Nietzsche said that you could measure the stature of a man by looking at his enemies. We are defined as much by our enemies as by our friends, as much by our negatives as by our positives. Just as the opposition between characters in a novel creates the drama, so a person's enemies give shape to the story of his life.

Enemies are dangerous because they consume energy and attention. Also, it's possible to become hypnotized by the thing we hate and stare at it for a lifetime. The energies of many societies and individuals are exhausted by hot and cold warfare. When being *against* becomes more important than being *with* or *for,* the enemy has destroyed the independence of your personality. The person who defines his existence as a battle against Communists, blacks, whites, the Establishment, Jews, women, abortionists, or Arabs forms a negative identity that indentures him to his enemy. A

I was angry with my friend;
I told my wrath, my wrath did end.
I was angry with my foe;
I told it not, my wrath did grow.
And I watered it in fears,
Night and morning with my tears.
And I sunned it with smiles,
And with soft deceitful wiles.
And it grew both day and night,
Till it bore an apple bright.
And my foe beheld it shine,
And he knew that it was mine.
And into my garden stole,
When the night had veil'd the pole;
In the morning glad I see;
My foe outstretched beneath the tree.
WILLIAM BLAKE,
"A Poison Tree"

Our spiritualization of hostility . . . consists in a profound appreciation of having enemies. . . . A new creation . . . needs enemies more than friends: in opposition alone does it feel itself necessary.

FRIEDRICH NIETZSCHE,
Twilight of the Idols

I went to school in the 1950s, and it was drilled into us from grammar school on. "Ain't" is bad, "aren't" is good. Communism's bad. Democracy's good. . . . In all my years in the army, I was never taught the Communists were human beings. We weren't in My Lai to kill human beings. We were there to kill ideology carried by—I don't know—pawns, blobs, pieces of flesh. I was there to destroy Communism. We never conceived of old people, men, women, children, babies.

LT. WILLIAM CALLEY

bad enemy destroys freedom, a good enemy provides the "loving combat" (Karl Jaspers) through which we can test and refine our values.

Viewpoints

One way we perpetuate conflict is by making our wars holy wars, our enemies the enemies of God. A nation declares *"Gott mit uns,"* "In God we trust," and pronounces its enemies atheistic barbarians who threaten the foundations of civilization. We often conduct personal battles from a similar stance of self-righteousness. But when we see our enemies as fallible human beings driven by self-interest (like ourselves), warfare becomes more humane—a matter of conflicting interests.

If you look at your life as a drama, what conflicts shape the action?

- What Big Enemies have you fought in defense of God, humanity, country, race, or creed? What happened when the battle was won? Or lost?
- What ideas, causes, or institutions have you championed? What was in it for you? Would you do it again?
- Who is the enemy on your horizon?
- Describe scenes in your life when you were consumed by anger or frozen in hatred. What did you do? Did it achieve the kind of result you would have liked?

The Vestal Virgin Warrior

I grew up on a Kentucky farm deep in the heart of the Bible belt, and Scripture flowed out of me like boogie beat. My body was a wreck due to infantile paralysis, pneumonia, and assorted other ailments until my high-school years when I began to train it into decent shape. When World War II broke out I wasn't planning to be a preacher anymore but I still believed "Thou shalt not kill." My father was ill and I had an automatic draft deferment to work his farm, but instead I went to Tennessee to write for a newspaper, determined to reflect the human face of America back to itself. But in 1941 I saw *Sergeant York* in a local movie house and everything turned around for me. York was a mountain man who shot a Sharps rifle and singlehandedly captured a company of German soldiers in World War I, all the while quoting the Epistle to the Romans on the necessity of combating the agents of the Devil. Because of Sergeant York's Christian dedication and my young reporter's quest to know (if I wasn't blessed with the answers, then I would spend my life asking the questions), I joined the Army at seventeen.

From then on I didn't get much sleep; I was pursuing Hitler's forces with the fiercest concentration. I was made a corporal in the artillery before I reached basic training and was assigned to intelligence and reconnaissance, which assured my position on the front lines. Once an officer watched me drill and suggested that I train at West Point but I declined, afraid of missing the holy war. In the spring of 1945 when we liberated a German concentration camp at Ohrdruf we found fresh stacks of machine-gunned Jews and Belgians. This was the terrible, conclusive proof that my crusade was on target. When the burgermeister from the next village was brought to Ohrdruf to look at what he had probably guessed but ignored, he hanged himself.

I trained myself like a precision lab instrument, effectively eliminating large quantities of the enemy by taking carefully calculated risks. I treated prisoners with a savagely cold courtesy and went to great lengths to harden myself to the dying. Once I ate my K-rations while sitting on the ass of a dead German. Another time, scouting in a wood with only a pistol, I came upon a GI sitting upright with his head blown off. He was still holding his rifle. I took it from his hands and thanked him out loud. He and I were intimate allies.

As soldier and forward observer I took a lot of personal risks and became something of a legend among the troops. They nicknamed me "Blood and Guts" after General Patton. The fact is, I loved combat with a kind of stupid

All that most maddens and torments; all that stirs up the lees of things; all truth with malice in it; all that cracks the sinews and cakes the brain; all the subtle demonisms of life and thought; all evil, to crazy Ahab, were visibly personified, and made practically assailable in Moby Dick. He piled upon the whale's white hump the sum of all the general rage and hate felt by his whole race from Adam down; and then, as if his chest had been a mortar, he burst his hot heart's shell upon it.
HERMAN MELVILLE, *Moby Dick*

If we could read the secret history of our enemies, we should find in each man's life sorrow and suffering enough to disarm all hostility.
HENRY WADSWORTH LONGFELLOW

innocence. I stayed on the lowest possible echelon of each maneuver in order to be in the front lines where there were no grays, no marginal considerations like food or status to worry about. The Army bureaucracy was so inept that it hardly ever reached the front lines, so we were free to fight our war the way we saw fit. My reputation for heroics paved my way; people expected king-sized deeds from me, and I delivered. The one or two times I shied away from taking the full, calculated risk I was miserable and ashamed. Nights I drank a lot, but always cemented myself together in the morning with calisthenics and oatmeal. Against the German enemy I could be totally committed, acting at the peak of my powers.

For me this was not a war of revenge. I was struggling to destroy an impersonal evil, not to inflict punishment. I stuck with God and prayed my way through scores of tight situations, repeating "Not my will but Thine be done" over and over again. If I repeated this prayer enough times I was able to relax and enjoy the battle. I was a vestal virgin warrior, an honest soldier who was dedicated to defeating God's enemy.

If you know the enemy and know yourself, you need not fear the result of a hundred battles.
SUN TZU

The officers in our Army who lived rigidly by the rulebook were usually the same ones who cracked under fire or wasted precious energies collecting battle souvenirs. I held such men in great contempt, and still do. Pomposity in journalism or science or government—living by form instead of purpose—is the dominant characteristic of my enemies. In my present work I spend a lot of time encouraging folks to play over their heads, to stop collecting souvenirs and rise to their own dreams. It's like the time I commanded a ground-survey team in a war zone and acted as the hot-coffee waiter. Since I didn't know any trigonometry myself, I toted a submachine gun with my wares so the men could work safely through the cold nights, and they did exceptional work. As their servant I was terribly proud of them. Ever since the war, people who rise full-hearted to the task of living have been my fighting allies.

—T GEORGE HARRIS is founder and (once again) editor of *Psychology Today*

PUNCTUATING TIME:
RITES OF PASSAGE

Timerunsonandonwithneverapauseorvariation, but human time is broken into manageable units. We create minutes, days, weeks, months, and years to punctuate the unbroken flow. We mark the beginning, middle, and end of things to find ourselves in time. Personal time is limited by the inevitability of death, so we invent clocks and anniversaries and holidays and decades to create the illusion of stasis in a fluid universe. We divide time to conquer it.

Our inner time sense records intensity and importance rather than duration: an October afternoon of love among the dunes may be written larger in memory than all the weeks surrounding it. When you put together the story of your life you face the central question of how to punctuate time. What moments will you isolate and give symbolic importance, single out for dramatic effect? To make a coherent story from the undifferentiated mass of your experience you need to divide the flow of time with a comma, a period, a paragraph, a section, a chapter.

Every person's autobiography is both unique and usual, the story of an individual life and of all mankind. We are shaped by an inescapable human condition which dictates certain events and themes that will figure prominently in every life story.

Most cultures create rites of passage to celebrate an individual's transition from one stage of life to the next. Baptism or circumcision may mark the passage from womb to membership in the tribe. Initiation ordeals or menstruation signal the end of adolescence and entrance into the adult world. Marriage and procreation may signify acceptance of mature responsibilities. And death is the doorway to heaven (or hell), oblivion, or rebirth.

The practice of ritualizing the standard divisions between the stages of life reflects an ancient wisdom about the care and management of crisis and trauma.

The multitude of men and women choose the less adventurous way of the comparatively unconscious civic and tribal routines. But these seekers, too, are saved—by virtue of the inherited symbolic aids of society, the rites of passage, the grace-yielding sacraments, given to mankind of old by the redeemers and handed down through millenniums.
JOSEPH CAMPBELL,
Hero with a Thousand Faces

The challenge is to learn to respond immediately to whatever it is time for.
SAINT BENEDICTINE
saying

Transitions are turbulent times. Sudden changes in body chemistry and social expectations—for instance at the onset of adolescence or toward the end of life—may cause radical changes in personality. The way an individual negotiates major identity crises depends to a large extent on how these crises are defined and valued by his society. If crisis is taken as a sign of sickness or disintegration the transitions will be accompanied by anxiety, loneliness, and shame. If they are seen as signs of growth they may be experienced with excitement and pride. For instance, primitive ordeals of initiation (fasting, endurance tests, the killing of an enemy or wild animal) focus adolescent anxiety on a task which can be performed with pride.

Perhaps the clearest indication of the dignity premodern societies afforded the transition crises is in the widespread tales of the journey of the hero. The hero—the dragon killer, shaman, Siddhartha, Christ, Orpheus—must face a radical loss and rediscovery of identity. The story is told in many idioms but always the hero forsakes comfort, security, and certainty when he plunges into the dark habitation of the powers of evil. While in the underworld he fights with a demon or devil, and is often crucified. But eventually he rises from the dead and returns to the ordinary world with enlightenment and power. In the hero legends the promise is clear: any person who dares the radical descent into the chaos that lies beneath the veneer of personality and civilization has a chance of returning with a whole soul.

In modern society the rites for marking the divisions between the stages of life are mechanical, ill-defined, or nonexistent. We don't punctuate clearly enough. Going to school is sometimes regarded as initiation into the community beyond the home. Sex or a job or a driver's license are the tokens of graduation into the initial stages of adult life. Credit cards and a mortgage are signs of the full responsibility of maturity. Between maturity and retirement we do not expect to have identity crises. Those persons who do have "nervous breakdowns," neuroses, or emotional illnesses are sent to psychiatrists or tranquilized; they are made to feel

As I moved from one man to the next I became aware of a subtle difference among them . . . Their company had killed . . . they had seen violent death for the first time and something of the cruelty combat arouses in men. Before the fire-fight those marines fit both definitions of the word infantry, *which means either a "body of soldiers equipped for service on foot," or "infants, boys, youths collectively." The difference was that the second definition could no longer be applied to them. Having received that primary sacrament of war, baptism of fire, their boyhoods were behind them.*

PHILLIP CAPUTO,
A Rumor of War

ashamed of their trauma. Our definition of the hero's journey as neurosis or psychosis adds guilt, loneliness, and despair to transitions which could be creative events.

Viewpoints

Discovering your identity, organizing your life story, punctuating your time involves dividing your life into stages.

- Choose ten scenes from your past which were important pivotal events in your life and describe them. Detail the circumstances, characters, and backgrounds of each scene. How are the scenes you have chosen representative of your present life? How did they change or affect you? How has your view of them altered over the years?
- Make an outline of your autobiography. What are the major divisions? Chapter titles? Subsections? The title of the book? What stages does your life naturally seem to fall into? What ages were "crisis" periods for you?
- When did you cease to be a child? When did you cease to be young? When did you become mature? When did you become old?
- What personal, family, and social rituals or celebrations were involved in changing stages?
- After you've done an initial outline of your autobiography, put it aside and do another that uses entirely different organizing principles, chapter titles, pivotal events, key persons, and time scales. Turn your story inside out; try a new way of punctuating your time. If your life story has the feel of a tragedy, flip it over and make it a comedy; if it sounds like a romance, change the tone slightly so that it is ironic; if it has a pathetic ring, turn it into a hero tale.
- How do you envision punctuating your time in the future?

Before entering marriage each Babylonian maiden was initiated into womanhood within the sanctity of the temple, sacrificing her maidenhood and experiencing the first fruits of her sexuality. The stranger, who was viewed as an emissary of the gods, came and threw coins into the lap of the woman of his choice and said, "May the goddess Mylitta make thee happy." . . . He did not pay for the woman, but gave to the goddess for allowing him to partake of her sacrificial rite. Both the act of love-making and the offering were dedicated and thus made holy.
NANCY QUALLS-CORBETT,
The Sacred Prostitute

I'm Glad I Don't Like Spinach

The Celebrant says to the woman: "Will you have this man to be your husband; to live together in the covenant of marriage? Will you love him, comfort him, honor and keep him, in sickness and in health; and, forsaking all others, be faithful to him as long as you both shall live?" The woman answers: "I will."
The Book of Common Prayer

I walked away from our campfire one night to go to the camp of the Bushmen. . . . Halfway between I saw against the star-sheen the figure of something. It was a woman, holding a child up to the stars and saying something. I whispered to my interpreter, "What's going on?" He said to me, "Well, that woman, she's asking the stars up there to take away from this child the heart of a child and give him the heart of a star." "Why the heart of a star?" "Because the stars are great hunters and she wants her little boy to have the heart of a hunter."
LAURENS VAN DER POST,
Patterns of Renewal

From the very beginning I was attracted to boys instead of girls, but I felt terribly guilty about it. I thought my feelings were dreadful, sinful, perverted; I was the only boy in the world who wanted the things I did. I was bad, bad, bad and would surely go to hell.

But when I was fourteen I broke through all that by making love with Howie—an older kid who lived down the street—and that one experience showed me what was natural to me. You read all kinds of stuff saying that a homosexual experience is a horrible thing for a young boy, it cripples him for life and so on. In my case, that wasn't the result. It was a pretty cataclysmic experience, but what I got out of it was a tremendous feeling of relief, you know; I found out I wasn't alone, that there were other people who liked what I did and therefore I couldn't be such a big sinner! After that "rite of passage" I felt tremendously at ease with my sexual feelings. I knew what I wanted, and I knew with whom too!

During that time Mother hung a light which was really an old tin lantern punched full of holes on the front porch. It didn't give much light and wasn't worth a damn, but Mother was quite pleased with it. I remember the day she showed it to my older brother. He looked at it and said, "It doesn't give much light, but it's probably good enough for Leon and Howie to sit out under at night!" I didn't know how much any of them knew during those years, but I did know that as long as I could go on doing as I pleased it didn't really matter.

I can't imagine what my life would have been like if I hadn't been gay. I just never think of it, it doesn't enter my head, though I'm sure I wouldn't like it! It's like that joke about the kid who said, "I'm glad I don't like spinach because if I did I'd *eat* the awful stuff!" I'm happy with my appetites the way they are, pretty much like I found them at fourteen.

—LEON is a gentleman from Virginia
who loves opera and American landscapes

Folks I Have Known and How They Moved Me

INTRODUCTION

I lost my father and my mother wasn't available much. So I grew up like a weed in whatever soil I found around me.

CHAPTER ONE: GRANDMA MURPHY

Grandma supervised my piano lessons, starched and ironed my dresses, and sent me to school with a powdered nose and Evening in Paris dabbed behind each ear. She was herself a perfect lady except for one quirk: Grandma had this huge mound of dried dog shit that she treasured like a rare gem. Usually she used it as a doorstop, but when the nuns came calling she always placed it smack in the center of the living-room rug.

Moral: Even perfect ladies have their idiosyncrasies.

CHAPTER TWO: SISTER PRUDENTIA

When a boy in my kindergarten class wet his pants and burst into tears Sister Prudentia called his parents. His mother and father came at once, kissed him, shook hands with the sister, and took the kid home with them. I thought it a wonderful scene and wet my chair the same afternoon. Even though I cried real tears Sister Prudentia would have none of it. She made me stay on the flooded chair the rest of the day. And after that I had to walk home from school with my skirt hanging wet in front of everyone.

Moral: What works for your brother may not work for you.

CHAPTER THREE: MRS. GARBEY

For a while my sister and brother and I lived in a boardinghouse. The managers used food for bribes and punishment, so I always felt a little bit hungry. One day my third-grade teacher, Mrs. Garbey, asked me to carry her lunch bag out to the garbage can. I did, and she asked me to do it every day after that. I would go directly into the girls' room and gobble up the fresh milk and sandwiches that were always in the brown bag. Mrs. Garbey never said a word about these extended missions, but soon there were cookies in the bag too.

Moral: (There isn't one. It's just that true gifts are always remembered.)

You've got the same body, with the same organs and energies that Cro-Magnon man had thirty thousand years ago. Living a human life in New York City or . . . in the caves, you go through the same stages of childhood, coming to sexual maturity, transformation of the dependency of childhood into the responsibility of manhood or womanhood, marriage, then the failure of the body, gradual loss of its powers, and death. You have the same body, the same bodily experiences, and so you respond to the same images.
JOSEPH CAMPBELL,
The Power of Myth

CHAPTER FOUR: GAIL HENLEY

The Henley family lived way outside of town and didn't believe in bathing for some reason, so Gail was the butt of many eighth-grade jokes. I set out to befriend her and gradually induced her to wash after gym class with soapy paper towels. But when Gail responded by inviting me to spend a weekend with her strange family I made up an excuse and backed off. I was scared of getting contaminated, and after that I felt too guilty to speak to her.

Moral: If you convert someone to the one true path, don't be shocked when she starts to identify with you.

CHAPTER FIVE: JOE DiMAGGIO

More than anything I wanted to be a boy and a professional baseball player. But the closest I ever came to it was the day Joe DiMaggio came to town and I touched his right buttock in a crowd. It was wonderful, but not magical. Finally I had to give up my dreams and resign myself to being a girl.

Moral: Society has plans for you long before you arrive.

CHAPTER SIX: SID BRESLIN

His friends said he was infatuated with me, but I just couldn't believe it. True, I was a pretty ornament on his arm, but I hadn't heard of half the titles on his bookshelves and felt abysmally average around him and his bright friends. I worried and hesitated too long, and finally he threw up his hands and I fell out. That's when I decided that it must have been love.

Moral: If you pay enough attention to your inferiority feelings they'll probably come true.

CHAPTER SEVEN: DUKE CLEVELAND

A quick look at his life story would tell you that the man had suffered. And a look at the long string of deluded women in his life would tell you that they'd suffered too. But I believed in his struggles and his causes, and in my ability to be different from the other women. I was wrong: I lost heart, weight, humor, and nearly my life before I got up

When a Bushman died they buried him with his face to the east, that is, in the direction from which the new day comes, and they buried him with some ostrich eggs full of water beside him for the long journey, with his bow and arrow and his spear. They piled the red sand over him, then they heaped wood at the foot of his grave and set fire to it. I said to them, "Why the fire?" and they answered, "Because it is dark where he is and he needs the light of the fire to show him the way to the day beyond."
LAURENS VAN DER POST, *Patterns of Renewal*

and walked away. It might have helped if we'd liked each other.

Moral: If you persist in confusing a person with a cause, they'll both run away with you.

EPILOGUE

My life has been full of sad, dramatic experiences. But I dread the pathos of it all, so I tend to break them down into quick, wry episodes. I'm probably afraid that if I let them drag on they will drag me down and turn other people off; humor is so much more appealing than heaviness. And yet, looking back with a laugh means that whole hunks of reality get edited out. My mother, for instance, hardly appears here, because she's pathetic enough to turn the whole thing into a tragedy. Still, the story is to be continued, and next time I do this I think I'll let more in and skip the moral conclusions: maybe by now the sorrow in my life can mix with the comedy without poisoning everything.

—MARJORIE is a psychotherapist living in the Southwest

You have got to own your days and name them, each one of them, every one of them, or else the years go right by and none of them belong to you.
HERB GARDNER,
A Thousand Clowns

5

THE FUTURE

You Are What You Want

Time shapes our present the way a sculptor shapes unworked clay, molding each moment between the right hand of the past and the left hand of the future. What we remember characterizes us as uniquely as our thumbprints. What has happened to us molds us as certainly as what has not. An amalgam of the known and the unknown, of fact and possibility, makes up what we call ourselves.

A few generations ago, planning for the future was *the* mark of maturity. During the 1960s and 1970s it became a little suspect: since no one knows what the future will be, young people said, why not live today and let tomorrow take care of itself? Today college students are turning in droves toward banking, computer science, and technological industries. Hard work, greed, and planning for a secure future are back in style.

But no matter how fashions change, only children can afford to live in an eternal now. Most of us have too many unsatisfied desires to be content with the moment. We want more than we now have. We demand of the future some imagined fullness that presently eludes us. We want to grow, to experience more, to be more. There is always something we want and don't have: a happy marriage, a Mercedes-Benz, a shack in the country, satisfying work. We chase absent satisfactions; surely, someday we will be nearer to perfection, to the furtive desires we have stored in tomorrow. Or will we?

What do we want? What fulfillment could satiate the desire that motivates human striving? Augustine thought the restless heart could find its peace only in God. Marx was certain it would find a homeland in the proletarian state. Freud suggested that our true desires are repressed and unconscious and we really want to return to the security of the womb. In our discontent we try to quiet desire with religion, romance, status, sensation, food, or fame, but we are never filled. The wanting remains.

The question is perennial: can desire be satisfied? Eastern philosophers and religious thinkers tend to believe that it cannot; Nirvana is found when desire is extinguished. Western psychologists are generally more pragmatic and optimistic. They work on the assumption that, if individuals can unmask their desires and discover what they are, they may achieve happiness.

If we unearth our unconscious desires and lay them alongside our conscious ones we can trace the anatomy of our desires and learn something about the source of our conflicts. Some desires can be fulfilled while others endure in the form of fantasies. Stories and myths help to excite and clarify them. Any mythical portrait which a culture projects (Buddha, Socrates, Jesus, Martin Luther King, Jr., John Wayne, Mother Teresa of Calcutta, or Jane Fonda) promises its imitators a satisfying style of life.

Fantasies, dreams, daydreams, and future plans are also excellent divining rods for locating underground desires. Our wildest and tenderest desires hide out in our imaginations, emerging when sleep, drugs, or strong feelings loosen the rational censorship we call common sense. When they emerge, dreams and desires tend to turn everything topsy-turvy. As Chuang-tze said: "Last night I dreamt I was a butterfly. Now I don't know whether I am a butterfly dreaming I am a man, or a man dreaming I am a butterfly." But when the voices that come in visions and dreams are welcomed, a new harmony sounds between the unconscious and the conscious.

History is simply man's desperate effort to give body to his most clairvoyant dreams.
ALBERT CAMUS,
Neither Victims nor Executioners

It is a Freudian axiom that the essence of man consists, not . . . in thinking, but in desiring.
N. O. BROWN,
Love's Body

Born to shop.
Bumper sticker

By the time s/he is 60 years old, the average American will have seen 50,000 ads and 350,000 television commercials.

DEATH: THE AWFUL CERTAINTY

The only event we can predict with virtual certainty is the one we least like to think about—our own deaths. Death is the doorway to the future, the one fact in a world otherwise governed by probabilities. Before we can fantasize freely about our futures we have to break the death barrier—confront the ambivalent feelings that cluster around our images of the end.

Modern people don't die; they just pass away. Soldiers take care of our killing and undertakers do our burying, preferably discreetly. Classical philosophers insisted that wisdom and happiness were only possible after a person had come to terms with the inevitability of death. Plato defined philosophy as training for dying. If we evade death we avoid the event that sets the definitive limits on our mortality; we cling to the illusion that there's an eternity of time in which to do the things we lack courage to do today. Death disillusions by reminding us that we arise from and return to the earth (humus). It makes us human by confronting us with the fragility of life and the need for decision.

For the human animal there is no purely biological act. Death (like birth or sex) is surrounded with interpretations and explanations. We need to understand what death means and why people should die. Throughout the course of history the myths, images, and metaphors used to interpret death reflect a profound ambiguity. It is never clear whether death is friend or enemy, the beginning or the end of life.

Either death is: an end to life; the ultimate enemy; the grim reaper; the castrator. In the Christian tradition, as in many ancient myths, death enters the world as a punishment for transgression against some divine law. Man dies because he ate the forbidden fruit or because he broke a taboo or stole fire from the gods. If there were no enmity between man and the gods, no alienation, there would be no death.

Or death is: a prelude to rebirth; the hidden friend;

Man is an animal that has to do something about his ephemerality. He wants to overcome and be able to say, "You see, I've made a contribution to life. I've advanced life, I've beaten death, I've made the world pure." But this creates an illusion. The dynamic of evil is the attempt to make the world other than it is, to make it what it cannot be, a place free from accident, a place free from impurity, a place free from death.

ERNEST BECKER

the womb of life; the lover. In cultures where the feeling for nature remains strong, human life is seen as analogous to the life of plants and death is viewed as one stage in an eternal cosmic cycle. In the winter of his life man dies in order that he may be reborn in the spring. The Hopi Indians symbolize this by burying their dead in the fetal position. In the end we come back to the beginning.

Different psychological realities underlie these two estimates of death. We experience death only as observers. A dying person experiences dying but, presumably, not death. The survivors observe a lifeless body and experience grief, relief, anger, and panic. To an observer death seems final. It steals away a unique person whose life can never be restored or repeated. If we have loved the dead person death seems the final enemy of love and life. When we think about our own death we are inundated by the images and fears that surround an imaginary future event. But we confront our feelings about death most directly when we come face to face with any radical change in our lives. Something in us (the ego, the infantile self, the first-born self) does not believe we can survive fundamental changes in personality structure or life circumstances, and so each crisis in life is shadowed by death. Then when we survive the crisis we realize that change may mean metamorphosis rather than death. The ego dies and a stronger self is born. Then it may come to us that death is only a gateway to wider life, the final trip beyond the prison of the ego.

Speculations and explanations always pale before the reality of death. In the end we have to face it raw. We can escape obsession with death by paying attention to the appeals of living. It is unlived life that makes fear of death persistent and morbid. We might even see our death as a gift to the living: nature decrees that the father dies so the child can inherit his full place in the sun. Even the death of those we love is not a total loss. Death adds the bass notes to the symphony. By our grief for what is missing we know the terrible value of what was once present among us.

Formerly men had no fire but ate all their food raw. At that time they did not need to die, for when they became old God made them young again. One day they decided to beg God for fire. They sent a messenger to God to convey their request. God replied to the messenger that he would give him fire if he was prepared to die. The man took the fire from God, but ever since then all men must die.
African myth

Death is the only wise adviser that we have. Whenever you feel that everything is going wrong and you're about to be annihilated, turn to your death and ask if that is so. Your death will tell you that you're wrong. . . . Your death will tell you, "I haven't touched you yet."
DON JUAN,
Journey to Ixtlan

Maybe the best we can do is struggle against death as if it were our final enemy, refuse to "go gentle into that good night," affirm the priority of light over darkness. Then, in that penultimate moment (when, it is said, our life flashes before us and we know that it was good), we may allow death to turn its other face toward us and know that it is a friend. Maybe.

Viewpoints

I am a Fox.
I am supposed to die.
I already threw my life
  away.
Something daring,
Something dangerous,
I wish to do.
ERDOES AND ORTIZ,
American Indian Myths and
Legends (Brule Sioux)

Two contrasting atti-
tudes toward death ap-
pear among the primi-
tive peoples of the world.
Among the hunting
tribes whose life style is
based on the art of
killing . . . death is a
consequence of violence
and is generally ascribed
not to the natural desti-
ny of temporal beings
but to magic. . . . For
the planting folk . . .
death is a natural phase
of life, comparable to the
moment of the planting
of the seed, for rebirth.
JOSEPH CAMPBELL,
Primitive Mythology

If you want to feel what death means to you, take a look at your favorite death fantasies.

- How do you most frequently see yourself dying?
- Who died the way you expect to die?
- What activities may dictate your style of dying? (Smoking, drinking, commuting, worrying, mining, skydiving?)
- When will you die? Who died at this age?
- Why are you going to die? Is death a failure? A depletion of energy? A natural conclusion to life? Do you die to make room for the living? Because your body is worn out? Because you are bored, frustrated, despairing? Because you are satisfied?
- What is your dominant attitude toward death—defiance, acceptance, fear, longing, sorrow, curiosity?

Imagine you died yesterday and look back on your life. You died with many dreams unfulfilled.

- What accomplishments, relationships, moments mean most?
- What are your regrets? What have you left undone that you wanted to do? What have you done that you wish you hadn't?

Death wears many faces. When the young die, death is tragedy; when the old or incurably ill die, it is deliverance; when our enemies die, it is retribution and justice.

- What moods and emotions have dominated your experience of the death of others? (Grief, anger, fear, relief?)
- Whose death would cause you the greatest sorrow? Whose would give you the greatest pleasure? Who would care the most if you died?

In the world of myth death is usually considered an unnatural event, a strangeness in need of an explanation. Here is an excerpt from *African Myths and Tales* (edited by Susan Feldmann) that tells why death came into the world.

Formerly men had no fire but ate all their food raw. At that time they did not need to die for when they became old God made them young again. One day they decided to beg God for fire. They sent a messenger to God to convey their request. God replied to the messenger that he would give him fire if he was prepared to die. The man took the fire from God, but ever since then all men must die.

- Make up your own myth about why we must die.

The Death Machine

It used to be that every time I drove on a freeway, death was right behind me. It was a silver Mercedes cutting into my lane; or a Mack truck barreling up from behind, squishing me like a blister; or sometimes an overpass would give way, burying me in great heaps of concrete. I was always at the wheel when these things happened, driving too fast, straining to outrun the Death Machine. . . . Later death stopped haunting the freeway and moved into the world of disease. Now I was losing great quantities of weight, or my blood was drying up, or my muscles caved in

One day God asked the first human couple, who then lived in heaven, what kind of death they wanted, that of the moon or that of a banana. God explained to them: the banana puts forth shoots which takes its place, and the moon itself comes back to life. The couple considered for a long time. If they elected to be childless they would avoid death, but they would also be very lonely and would not have anybody to work and strive for. Therefore they prayed to God for children. Since that time man's sojourn is short on this earth.

African myth

on April 1. Everyone else was terribly shocked, but once I felt death pumping through my veins, I let go easily. I saw myself turn to the wall, dying with my eyes open.

Which brings me to suicide, my secret death. That fantasy comes in two versions. One suicide is a crazed plea for attention, a calculated demand that the world pay for my frustrations. In this fantasy I can't quite die: death spits me back, leaving me with ugly scars, stunned friends, and another perspective. The other suicide is a clean, active ending, a match I carry in my pocket in case of a blizzard, my way of assuming (or presuming) as much power over my death as I have in my life. I detect the fingers of that fantasy in a lot of literature. Camus finally drove into a tree, Virginia Woolf walked into water, Mayakovsky blew his head off, Sylvia Plath opened the gas oven and left a note for the maid. Suicide seduces me with its drama and relief, but at the same time it's terribly sad, a robber. I wish those artists were still around heating up the world.

And then I think of Picasso, running up and down stairs and making perfect paintings until he was ninety-one, and I know there are active ways of living as well as dying. The fact is, most of the time when I want to die it's because I'm not as *alive* as I want to be and death would at least blot the disappointment. My freeway deaths have to do with feeling desperately competitive and overpowered (high gear ain't good enough); death by disease is final proof that we're nothing but victims in a deadly world. That ending lets me off the hook. It says, "See? Why fight and love and work when it all can be canceled in an instant!"

But when I step back and look at my bones and my luck and my string of octogenarian relatives I see that I'm probably destined (doomed, maybe) to live a long life. It's not as if I'm royalty threatened by court intrigues, or some rare, frail beauty too sensitive to stay alive. At eighty (knock on wood!) I'll probably be rocking on a porch somewhere, watching the young folks slugging it out, creaking toward senility, my old crone death rocking away beside me.

—DAISY is a single mother and artist

The earliest evidence of anything like mythological thinking is associated with graves. . . . Burials always involve the idea of the continued life beyond the visible one, of a plane of being that is behind the visible plane. . . . I would say that is the basic theme of all mythology—that there is an invisible plane supporting the visible one.
JOSEPH CAMPBELL,
The Power of Myth

If You're on Your Way to the Morgue

Death can belt you pretty hard, but if you're done loving somebody, it's nothing but a trip to the morgue.

The day I went to the D.C. morgue to identify my husband's body I couldn't even find the place. I was looking for a cool gray tomb like all the rest of those official buildings but none of them matched the number they'd told me over the phone. Finally I flagged a cab and the driver (a real nice-looking man with smooth dark skin) nearly dropped his teeth. "Why lady," he said, "the morgue's just around the corner!" We were both laughing about mislocating the morgue just because it was bright red brick like a Methodist church, and then the cabby says, "If you're on your way to the morgue, how come you're so happy?"

Well, I was laughing because I once did love my man, I knew when I had it and I knew when it was gone. Before we were married he was gentle and respectful as any man I'd ever met. I wouldn't sleep with him before we were married but he didn't leave me. He just went on working hard and taking me to movies until I got good and ready to hitch up. But after that everything changed. He started putting down a lot of beer, and then other stuff, stepping out with women and hollering at me when I asked him about it. One day while I was ironing he stormed in, grabbed the iron, and laid it steaming hot on my upper arm. Well, I couldn't love that man anymore. I couldn't even recognize him. I kicked him out of the house and that was that.

I gave the driver a dollar, gathered up my nerve, and went into the morgue. A fat man with a beltful of keys (I guess he was caretaker of all those drawers of dead bodies) led me to room 127. He stood there rolling out my husband's chilled corpse, looking bored as anything. I was standing maybe ten feet away and couldn't get a good look at the dead man's face but I said, "Yeah, that's him," turned on my heel, and got the hell out of there.

I'll tell you this: I sure hope it *was* John Carter Lockwood lying there dead. If not, some poor lady's gonna be worrying her head for nothing, and I'm likely to end up living that bad dream all over again!

—A WOMAN IN HER SIXTIES who spoke
openly with us on a bus bench

Death is swallowed up in victory. O death, where is thy sting? O grave, where is thy victory?
ST. PAUL,
Corinthians

Let children walk with Nature, let them see the beautiful blendings and communions of death and life, their joyous inseparable unity, as taught in woods and meadows, plains and mountains and streams of our blessed star, and they will learn that death is stingless indeed, and as beautiful as life. . . . All is divine harmony.
JOHN MUIR, as quoted by Frederick Turner in *Rediscovering America*

Who's Worrying?

From the scientific point of view, death is a question without an answer, and therefore it is not a valid concern. In the broader sense, there really isn't any death. Atoms persist. Just as the car I'm driving has some molecules of steel that were probably once running around in a 1936 Ford, some of the carbon atoms in my body will exist in some other body later on. But that mechanism won't be me. You see, what is me? Me is only my present consciousness. I exist only as a series of metabolic connections in the brain that call up certain experiences in retrospect, perceiving an order that will someday disappear.

For some reason which we don't understand there has to be a beginning and an end to things. If all the mutants that ever lived were still alive you would have one hell of a situation! Death is simply a natural part of the life cycle. One hundred fifty years from now everyone who lives today will be gone, all 4.5 billion of us, and what will matter?

Death is only important to youth, who are attracted to the things they haven't done yet, or to people who are frustrated in their work and don't want to cash in until they at least get some pleasure out of life. But people who are involved in what really gives them pleasure just don't have that fear. When I'm solving theorems I'm not worrying about anything. What's important is the minimization of pain and the optimization of local pleasure.

Death is an abstract thing, almost as abstract as life itself. I'll probably never have to experience my own death. I am not the same person I was five years ago. I'm in a constant state of metamorphosis, so that my life is not a precipitous thing. And when I reach old age (if I do) one of two things will happen: I will go quickly or I will have evolved into senility or senescence, in which case I won't be me. For all I know, that old man will welcome death. I don't want it now but if I dropped dead tomorrow it wouldn't bother me. If it happens it happens. It's not something I think about. I'm concerned with the next moment, with what I can do tomorrow.

You mean other people really worry about death?

—MIKE is an engineer for an
aeronautics corporation and is nearing retirement

What makes dying easier is to be able to transcend the world into some kind of religious dimension. I would say that the most important thing is to know that beyond the absurdity of one's life, beyond the human viewpoint, beyond what is happening to us, there is the fact of the tremendous creative energies of the cosmos that are using us for some purposes we don't know. To be used for divine purposes, however we may be misused, this is the thing that consoles . . . I think it is very hard for secular men to die.
ERNEST BECKER
(terminally ill, just before his death)

THE ART OF FANTASY

Imagination is an incorrigible child forever at play with frivolities when reason is doing serious work. Daydreams wander in and out of consciousness, interrupting concentrated thought. As rationality gains exclusive control over our lives we drive out our daydreams. They are flights from reality into fancy, trips taken at the expense of the boss, the job, the problem that has to be solved. All true. Daydreams deliver us into the private world of unfulfilled desire and let us taste forbidden pleasures that are sweeter than work, duty, responsibility, honor, gentility, and moderation. They are disturbers of the peace, but we ignore them at our own peril. Without them the psyche shrivels.

The more we know about the kaleidoscopic worlds of desire the more we are likely to be able to make satisfying choices. Desires range from split-second spasms to lifelong intentions. Some desires lead to action; others linger or wear themselves out in fantasy. Imagine a scale of desire. The weakest desires are fleeting wishes, such as: "I wish I could fly, change sexes for a week, eat chocolate every day . . ." Wants are one degree stronger than wishes: "I really want to have a baby, write a book, learn to ski." Willing and deciding are manifestations of even stronger desires: "I probably won't become President but I will write a book." Action is the final stage in the realization of desire: "I decided to write and am typing this paragraph." There is no reason to assume that all desires must end in action, but it is helpful to know which of our wishes to ripen into wants, which wants to deepen into decisions, and which decisions to finally actualize.

Fantasy can be an economical way of trying on alternative ways of feeling, acting, and being. In the safety of the imagination we can become Charles Manson and purge our murderous rage without shedding blood, or make love to anyone without the entanglement of an actual relationship, or play God

Desire is the root of the universe. From Desire all things are born. Primordial matter and all beings are reabsorbed again through Desire. Without Shiva and Shakti creation would be a mere illusion. Without the action of Desire there would be no life, no birth and death.
SHILPA PRAKASHA

The extinction of desire
(Buddhism) or detach-
ment—or amor fati—
or desire for the absolute
good—these all amount
to the same: to empty
desire . . . of all content,
to desire in the void, to
desire without any wish-
es. To detach our desire
from all good things and
to wait. Experience
proves that this waiting
is satisfied. It is then we
touch the absolute good.
SIMONE WEIL,
Gravity and Grace

without having to reckon with the Devil. In fantasy any outlawed or unacceptable wish can find fulfill-ment. We can be as cruel, crazy, strong, weak, grandi-ose, timid, or whimsical as we please.

Paradoxically, when we stay in touch with our most outrageous fantasies our path toward realistic goals is most direct. When we allow the child within us free play it is easier to enjoy our self-chosen responsibili-ties.

Viewpoints

Your fantasy life can tell you much about your unfulfilled wishes. Discover where your mind wanders when it slips away from grim reality. The next time you're stuck in a meeting or a concert hall and can't concentrate, let your fantasies fly and watch where they go. (Are you killing the boss? Eating? Mediating world peace? Being applauded? Winning someone over to your side?) If you don't force your daydreams into rational or moral categories they will take you fantastic places.

Planned fantasy trips are another way of exploring the imagination. Try these archetypal scenes.

The primary imagina-
tion I hold to be the living power and prime
agent of all human per-
ception, and as a repeti-
tion in the finite mind
of the eternal act of creation in the infinite
I Am.
SAMUEL TAYLOR
COLERIDGE

- While hiking in the mountains you notice a cave in a wall of granite. You crawl up to the opening and look into the darkness. In the distance you hear running water and a voice calling, "Let me out. Let me out." And . . .
- On an average morning in early May you receive a letter informing you that Donald Trump plans to leave you his entire estate. After recovering from the shock (and calculating the amount that would be left after taxes) you decide that the first thing you'll do is . . .
- Create a sexual fantasy in which you are totally satisfied.

- Imagine that you can travel freely inside your body in the manner of Isaac Asimov's *Fantastic Voyage*. Walk through your body and describe what you see.
- You accidentally take a drug that erases all inhibitions and morality for one week, along with your accountability. You are perfectly free. What do you do for seven days?
- You are invisible for a few days. What do you do?

Design a utopian society that could conceivably exist in your future.

- How is society governed?
- What are the sexual, religious, and political mores?
- Who works? When? For what?
- How and by whom are children raised and educated?

Play God and make this the best of all possible worlds.

- What do you change, and what remains the same? (Are there time and space? Are there human beings? Minds? Bodies? Is there pain? Tension? Death?)
- What do creatures live for?

Without this playing with fantasy no creative work has ever yet come to birth. The debt we owe to the play of imagination is incalculable.
C. G. JUNG

Life Could Be a Dream

Playing God is an old role for me; I already tried it on and failed. When I was seventeen I figured out there wasn't any God and decided to become a scientist. If there's no God and no absolute values, what is there except survival? So I made up my mind to work on the problem of aging. I knew that immortality was a farfetched idea but science was our one hope so I ran after it anyway. I zoomed through the biology doctoral program and went right to work for a prominent research foundation. By the time I was twenty-five I was considered an expert on the science of aging but it was beginning to look like a poor proposition; I began to suspect that aging was not a disease that was likely to be cured in my

Where there is no vision the people perish.
Proverb

Iroquois Dream Event I:
After having a dream,
let someone else guess
what it was. Then have
everyone act it out to-
gether.

Iroquois Dream Event II:
Have participants run
around the center of a
village, acting out their
dreams and demanding
that others guess and
satisfy them.
JEROME ROTHENBERG,
Shaking the Pumpkin

I have a dream that my
four little children will
one day live in a nation
where they will not be
judged by the color of
their skin, but by the
content of their char-
acter.
MARTIN LUTHER KING,
JR.

lifetime. And to complicate matters further, I discovered people. I fell in love and saw that beauty is mixed in with mystery and that the universe is much more complex than my logical positivist training allowed for. Reality can't be caught in a net of Euclidian logic and verifiable hypotheses. At the ripe old age of twenty-seven I left the aging business and began to explore mortality.

Now I'm not sure I like the idea of being God, it's too much responsibility and gravity. But if I *was* God I'd make some changes. First I'd wipe out cruelty. I'd be like a benign General Motors recalling defective models, eliminating all those people who spend their lives making war or making other people miserable. Basic structures like time, space, sex, bodies, and Chicago could remain much as they are; the main thing I'd do is take the load off people by teaching them to separate their bodies from their souls. Right now I know we are spirits, but I'm not sure we could exist without bodies. If we could, everything would be possible. We could park our bodies, take an astral flight, and come back for them later. We could take little trips inside other people's minds and see how they worked without losing our own identities. And unless we bogged down in pride or stubborn-ness, we'd never have to get stuck in outer space, in the grave, in Anaheim, California, or even in love.

If people could only be taught to separate body and soul, life would be like a dream. The dream world is a great place because if you know you're dreaming you can go ahead and enjoy the action without being responsible for the conse-quences. You just wake up and poof! it's all gone. The other night I (not God now but me, the mortal) had a fantastic dream like that. I'm riding my bicycle down the Seventh Street hill and can't control the damn thing. It won't brake, won't quite steer, and it looks like I'm going to crash over the cliff at the end. I'm panicked trying everything I can think of to get control until suddenly I realize I'm in a dream. Then I think: if I'm in a dream I can't get killed, and it's not every day that I get a chance to ride my bike over a cliff! So I let go of the brakes and relax. I expect to drop down the cliff and break some bones maybe, but when I hit the first landing the bike bounces up and soars off over the ocean! If I was God I'd teach people to sit back and enjoy their flights!

But I'm not so sure about death anymore: maybe life wouldn't be so rich if we didn't think this was our only trip. I guess what I'd do if I was God is let people avoid their deaths (indefinitely, but not forever) by being able to leave their bodies at will. Meanwhile, human minds would inevitably be devising more and more fantastic tricks for themselves, which would keep us all entertained. Life on earth would be rich as a dream—and *almost* eternal!

—FRED is a high-tech entrepreneur
and self-made millionaire

DREAMS

In dreams we live a thousand lives. When sleep conquers reason we become omnipotent; like Proteus, we change form to experience the beasts and little children that roam within us.

We are such stuff as dreams are made on, and our little life is rounded with a sleep.
WILLIAM SHAKESPEARE,
The Tempest

Psychology has rediscovered what ancient and primitive peoples knew: that dreams are essential for sanity. Greek seers, Roman emperors, and Egyptian pharaohs used dreams to decipher the future. Many American Indians consulted dreams to learn when they should feast or take to the warpath. Job thought that dreams were songs God gave us in sleep. Freud saw them as the royal road to the unconscious. Recent experiments have shown that persons deprived for several nights of the part of sleep in which dreaming takes place become anxious and disassociated. A healthy human mind seems to operate on two levels, the realistic and the fantastic, the conscious and the unconscious. Like a live virus, the chaos of playful fantasy inoculates us against serious madness.

Most of us pay sparse attention to the one-third of our lives we live in sleep. The rationality that dominates our culture is concentrated on conquering the outer world, thrusting toward craters on the moon. When volcanoes erupt in our inner spaces we label them emotional disturbances, or psychotic episodes, and try to seal them off with tranquilizers or therapy.

Modern culture is permeated by a deep, unspoken moralism that is evident in our suspicions of the free lunch, free association, free schools, and free dreams.

Whenever the unconscious is opened up, whether by psychoanalysis, psychedelic drugs, or exaggerated attention to dreams, there is danger of getting stuck in memories of ancient injuries or staying forever among the lotus-eaters feeding on the nectar of fantasies. The inward journey is most enriching for the traveler who brings the visions of the night into the light of day.

Viewpoints

Old Man said to the people: "Now, if you are overcome you may go to sleep, and get power. Something will come to you in your dream that will help you. Whatever these animals tell you to do, you must obey them, as they appear to you in your sleep. Be guided by them."
Blackfoot Lodge Tales

Dreams are like people: they respond to attention and retreat when neglected. Keep a notebook by your bed and write down as many of your dreams as you can. If you wake in the night assume the position you were in while dreaming and sink back into semisleep. Keep the scenes you remember from the dream on the edge of your awareness and the whole thing may revive. With practice you can learn to recall panoramic dreams in full living color. Save a few minutes before going to sleep and before getting up to simmer in bed; the timeless area between waking and sleeping is particularly fertile for cultivating dreams.

Here are some dreaming clues:

- Dreams are mysteries which nobody knows how to interpret. Theories about why we dream and what dreams mean are only theories. Dreams may be waste products of the mind, voices of the dead, solutions to crossword puzzles, or flashes from the future.
- Enjoy your dreams. At the very least they are playthings of the mind. If you assign them a single meaning they are likely to evade you.
- Share your dreams. They are free gifts, so why not pass them on?
- Who appears in your dreams? How often? Why do you think they are there?

- There is no complete interpretation of any part of a dream. If you dream that you're riding a horse down a woody path with serpents circling your body it may symbolize desire for sex, or freedom, or greater control over wild instincts. Or someone may be rocking the bed. All or none of these things may be true. Play with different possible meanings.
- Interpret one dream in the light of others. Look for symbols and themes that appear over a long period of time. A series of dreams about cops or caves will add force and clarity to your understanding of what these things symbolize for you.
- Cultivate an active relationship to your dreams. If a dream disturbs you or feels unfinished, decide to dream it again and see where it goes. Sometimes this works.
- Everything in a dream is a creation of your mind, a projection of some aspect of your personality (e.g., if your mother appears in a dream she may represent the maternal part of yourself). Fritz Perls, one of the creators of Gestalt therapy, suggested that we turn our dreams into psychodramas in which we play the role of every character or aspect. *I am an old house, I am barren, without ornament or beauty. I sit in the middle of a lonely field by myself. No one visits me anymore. . . . Be* each element in your dream.
- Pay special attention to recurring scenes, childhood dreams, and the most frightening and pleasant dreams you can remember.

Stars, darkness, a lamp, a phantom, dew, a bubble, a dream, a flash of lightning, or a cloud: Thus should one look upon the world.
"The Diamond-Cutter Sutra," Buddhist text

House of Horrors (A Dream)

I'm in the front room of a huge old layered house. There's a woman with dark skin and short dark hair standing by the window. She's wearing a plain black skirt and a white babydoll blouse that sticks out in front because she's pregnant. I've never seen her before. I go up to her and start kicking and shoving, gently at first and then harder. She doesn't fight back and I keep it up, prodding her from room to room. Finally she locks herself in the downstairs bathroom and suddenly there are three or four faceless people with me outside the door. I know she's trapped in there and, sure enough, we bust the lock with no trouble. The woman is standing in the corner by the tub. I say to the others, "Let's give it to her," and we start beating her savagely. I keep punching her belly with my fist, over and over, and she just stands there with her eyes closed, her arms flapping like rags in the wind. I open the medicine cabinet and take out five pairs of miniature scissors with sharp, tiny legs and hand them out to everyone. Between punches we poke them into her upper body. Every place we sink them two little red pools of blood appear on the soft white cotton in perfect circles, and I think it's pretty, I like watching them rise slowly to the surface. All this time the woman just pushes us back gently; she's taking it, just taking it. Eventually we whip her back into the front room. We're getting ready to leave, so I tell the lackeys to tie her into the chair with a piece of rope. Then she speaks and asks if I will please tie her lying on the sofa so that she can bear her child. Then for the first time I think about the consequences—the human consequences—of this thing. How will she get the kid out or cut the umbilical cord if her hands are tied? I tell the others, "Tie her on the sofa with her arms free, turn out the lights, lock all the doors, and yank out the phone." Then I take off, leaving everybody behind. I'm running down the street trying to get far away.

—HANNAH is an unmarried woman living
in the Northwest

House of Horrors Revisited
(A Psychodrama)

FRIEND: Assume that your dream is a drama between the different parts of yourself. Get inside the characters and let them talk to each other. First be the tormentor, the one you call "I."

TORMENTOR TO MOTHER: We're beating you and stabbing you all around your soft white heart and you pretend it isn't happening, you don't respond. Why don't you fight back? If you would respond maybe we would stop tormenting you. *(Mother keeps silent.)*

TORMENTOR TO BABY: And you, so protected in there, all curled up riding on somebody else; it'll be different when you come out! But it's your mother I'm really after, not you. She's so self-righteous, so silent.

MOTHER TO TORMENTOR: I don't know why you're doing this. I don't even know you. But this will pass. . . . It's like childbirth, if I can hold myself together I know it will pass. . . . You can't destroy the life in me.

FRIEND: Say that again.

MOTHER: You can't destroy the life in me. You can't destroy the life in me! You can hurt me but you can't destroy the life that's in my body. The only way you can touch that is by killing me and you won't do that, you're too small, you don't care enough to kill me, so all I have to do is endure. I have something you don't have, that's why you're doing this. You think the pools of blood are pretty because you've never had anything beautiful inside yourself. I hardly feel what you're doing to me: I'm thinking about my child and when she starts coming there's nothing any of you can do, you're just bringing it on faster, you're bringing my child out, which is what I want.

God gives us songs in our sleep.
JOB

FRIEND: Your voice is so weak and childlike that it cancels the force of what you're saying. Try being the baby in the womb; let yourself go all the way into feelings of passivity.

BABY: It's so nice and soft and thick and warm in here. There's some pressure from the outside but it doesn't hurt me, it feels like a liquid massage. Still, I think they're trying to get me to come out of here, and I don't want to.

FRIEND: Well, tell them so.

BABY TO TORMENTOR: Stop pressuring me. Go away and leave me alone, we have nothing to do with each other. Why shouldn't I stay in here? If I come out I'll just be like you, flailing and empty. . . . My mother wants me out so she can hold me, but that can't last long. *(Voice dim, fading)* I want to stay in here. . . .

TORMENTOR: You can stay in or come out, it makes no difference to me. *(Small laugh)* You're just a blob, something to watch. I don't care about you, I don't even care about your mother. I'm only beating her because she refuses to respond.

FRIEND: You still say these things with a child's voice. Do you really want the mother to respond?

DREAMER: She won't, I know she won't, from the beginning I knew she wouldn't. I guess that's why this whole thing feels so stifling: it's not in anybody's interest to move.

FRIEND: Then let the characters tell each other why it's not in their interest to communicate, why they won't be moved.

TORMENTOR TO MOTHER: You're a very smart lady. *(Big voice)* I guess that's why I'm trying to get you. You know that if you respond—if you kick or bite or scream—you'd start to feel more, and we'd start to feel guilty and want to shut you up and then we'd really have to hurt you, kill you maybe. It's better for the kid and for you not to show any feeling. But the beating goes on because we can't really get our hearts into it when you don't respond, there's no satisfaction, we're just going through motions. It's not really much fun, it's not even pretty, it's not anything. It's just something creepy happening in the corner of a bathroom.

MOTHER TO TORMENTOR: You don't move me. I know you're trying to hook me into your game—your street game—and maybe if I was by myself—if I was empty and bored like you—I would fight back if only to forget the pain. But I have something soft and strong in me and all of you are nothing, you don't even live here. I can be still because I know where I am.

FRIEND: Aha! So the dramatic conflict is between someone who's empty of life and someone who's full of it. Develop those two characters a little.

DREAMER: *(Long silence)* I am full of life. *(Dull voice)* There's something big inside me. It has its own heartbeat.

FRIEND: Be the heartbeat.

DREAMER: *(Irritated at friend)* I don't know how to be a heartbeat. I don't *feel* these things. . . .

FRIEND: You mean you *won't* be a heartbeat?

DREAMER: *(Angry, plaintive)* I don't know what you want from me. You'd like to see me roll around like a baby and admit that I'm just a baby. Well, why should I do that? Why should I admit that I'm a baby? It's enough that I am one.

FRIEND: Pretend you are me and answer that question.

DREAMER AS FRIEND: Why are you so afraid of being a baby? We all know you need protection, you're soft and

Everyman is me, I am
his brother.
No man is my enemy.
I am Everyman
and he is in and of me.
This is my faith,
my strength,
my deepest hope,
and my only belief.
KENNETH PATCHEN

The dream is the royal
road to the unconscious.
SIGMUND FREUD

mushy, you're mostly heartbeat. Why don't you just accept reality?

FRIEND: Now see if you can allow yourself to be the baby.

DREAMER AS BABY: I hate reality. I am not strong. If I have to be carried I'd rather be alone and in the dark. *(Beginning to weep)* When I was in the womb I was strong; after that it was all downhill. And that's because when I came out *I didn't care,* I didn't believe in anyone else. That's why acting out your dreams is crazy. Life is all acting anyway, so why act about acting? It just proves the absurdity of everything out here. Yeah, I'm an infant; I don't like being alive, it's second rate, just *being here* takes so much work. It would be better to be a rock or a tree, something that didn't have to pretend all the time. That's it: I feel like I have to pretend everything! Pretend to feel, pretend to be different, pretend to be the same, pretend to love, pretend to be happy. Human beings are so pathetic, we spend our whole lives trying to mold things into something else. I'd rather be a simple animal—not the kind that sticks scissors in people—but one that crawls cleanly around on its belly. I popped out of the womb a disappointed old lady and I don't think there's anything to do about it. *(Sobbing)* Inside there's one tiny seed and the rest is just clothing, layers and layers and layers. Jesus! All this energy spent learning how to accept the world we're born into, what could be more unnatural? And how can I ever feel very close to anyone? We start out in the dark and that's the way it stays. I guess all life starts out in a shell or a seed or a root or something, but other animals don't try to pretend, they don't go around beating their chests saying, "We're here and we're so special!" It's all so terrible, and so exhausting. . . .

FRIEND: You've gone all the way into the weak, sad, baby-victim half of your dream. Now see if you can come out and get into the strong, aggressive feelings of power you had as the tormentor. Knock that baby out of her passivity.

DREAMER AS TORMENTOR: Babies aren't human beings, they're just babies. Women exist to have babies, mothers live for babies, babies are the essence of everything. This whole world is a hive of grown-up babies. I don't want to be a baby. I put myself through years of strict training to avoid infancy, why throw it away now? When I die and they do an autopsy they'll see how I ground down my teeth and

The dream is the small hidden door in the deepest and most intimate sanctum of the soul, which opens into that primeval cosmic night that was soul long before there was a conscious ego and will be soul far beyond what a conscious ego could ever reach.
C. G. JUNG,
The Portable Jung

*Hold fast to dreams
For if dreams die
Life is a broken
winged bird
That cannot fly.*
LANGSTON HUGHES

strained my muscles trying to be an adult and they'll say, "Huh! What a surprise! We thought she was one of us, a real leader. . . ."

FRIEND: Okay, be a leader, a non-baby, a super-adult.

DREAMER AS LEADER: I'm a leader because *I know how to make people believe in what nobody believes in.* The rest of you are weak, you need me to keep you going because if you stop you'll quit. You must never let down your momentum, never. . . . But good leaders have to be personally believable, so I keep a lot of pressure on myself, I have to stay alert in order to keep the rest of you from losing heart. That's the human-being conspiracy: "If you'll be a leader, we'll be believers." Leaders probably never really believe themselves, which is why they are dependent on their followers.

FRIEND: That's exactly the same split you have in the dream. There are leaders (feelingless people who poke others in order to believe they are alive) and babies (weak, passive creatures who want to be left alone). These two extremes of your personality don't talk to each other, which is why they come out in your dreams. You hurt yourself in order to believe things that are only half real for you, right?

DREAMER: *(Voice soft but clear)* Yeah. I work hard at it. That's the really nightmarish part: *things don't come naturally to me,* you know, easy feelings like it's good, you're good, I'm good, everything's all right, it's a gift to be born. . . . I remember lying in bed at night when I was eleven or twelve, making hard little militant pacts with myself about working harder, being a better leader, not showing any human weaknesses, putting on a better show for the others, rising to the occasion and on and on. . . . I guess the hardest thing in the world for me is to be gentle with myself, to hold myself in my own arms. . . .

—HANNAH

A dream is a personal experience of that deep dark ground that is the support of our conscious lives, and a myth is the society's dream. The myth is the public dream and the dream is the private myth.
JOSEPH CAMPBELL,
The Power of Myth

SUFFERING: FATE AND FREEDOM

What you might do tomorrow depends on whether there is a tomorrow. Some theories of time and personality hold that tomorrow happened yesterday. Others say it is still to come.

Maybe: time is a circle; the future will repeat the past; there is nothing new under the sun; by the time we are five we have been programmed so totally that we can never erase the patterns on our brains; freedom is just another word for accepting what is inevitable; change is an illusion; growth is an orderly way of dying; history is a record that plays over and over again. . . .

Or maybe: time is an arrow; the future is open to radically new possibilities; by their actions human beings can create, cause change; freedom is the awful capacity to make the future different from the past; change is always possible; growth is an orderly way of living; history is a path into . . .

The catch is in the maybe. You have at least two theories to choose between. That means choosing how free you are. You have to decide whether you can decide to change and by your decision you will create one world or another and determine whether tomorrow has already happened.

There is a certain security in thinking that nothing new can happen. It gives confidence that the past provides ready-made models for dealing with every situation; you already have the needles you need with which to knit future experience. If everything is determined, life may be a trifle boring ("I have measured out my life with coffee spoons"—T. S. Eliot) but we at least escape the terrors of history. But if the future is open to novelty, tomorrow is an adventure that may turn out better—or worse—than yesterday. Then, like gypsies, our security is in our ability to survive on the open road.

If we are not free to change there is no future to talk about, so let's assume that change is possible, and look at the factors in personality that make it difficult.

When we see ourselves doing the same self-destructive things year after year it's easy to become disillusioned about the possibility of change. Same games. Same mistakes. Why do we sometimes feel perverse

Of all existing things some are in our power, and others are not in our power. In our power are thought, impulse, will to get and will to avoid, and in a word, everything which is our own doing. . . . What disturbs men's minds is not events but their judgments on events. . . . Ask not that events should happen as you will, but let your will be that events should happen as they do, and you shall have peace.
EPICTETUS

pleasure in the pain we cause ourselves by repeating destructive habits?

Masochism is loving the pleasure in pain. It is the clue to why we "rather bear those ills we have than fly to others that we know not of" (Shakespeare, *Hamlet*). We like to think that masochism is limited to perverted personalities, but most of us have at least one room in the mansion of our personality devoted to self-torture. Consider the mental anguish involved in small worries, anxieties, continual self-doubts; in the slow suicide of chronic anger or depression; in addiction to work, the more righteous sacrifice made on the altar of the "bitch-goddess, Success" (William James). Perhaps the majority of human suffering is self-imposed.

A story from Charles Lamb gives a clue to the mystery of self-imposed pain. Once upon a time in ancient China a house burned down, with a pig inside. While poking around the ashes the villagers came upon the roasted pig and began to sample this new delicacy. Captivated by the delicious taste, they got another pig, put it in another house, and set that house afire. Early in life we learn that pleasure accompanies otherwise destructive or painful conduct. When we are sick, we are rewarded with attention; when we bypass pleasure for duty, we are praised; when we are docile and obedient, we are loved. We learn early that the betrayal of our inner feelings and desires is often the price of social acceptance. Change happens once we learn that it is possible to have roast pig without burning down a house. Pleasure is a gift that doesn't necessarily depend on sacrifice.

It takes courage to admit that we have created much of our suffering, and to take steps to dismiss it. Strength and tenderness are needed for us to tolerate happiness.

Man can will nothing unless he has first understood that he must count on no one but himself; that he is alone, abandoned on earth in the midst of his infinite responsibilities, without help, with no other aim than the one he sets himself, with no other destiny than the one he forges for himself on this earth.

JEAN-PAUL SARTRE,
Nausea

Viewpoints

The pleasure we get from suffering is one of our most carefully guarded secrets. We like to deny the payoffs of pain. Like Prometheus, we blame the gods and ignore our complicity in creating our fate. See what happens when you reverse your story and take total responsibility for your sorrows.

- In what ways do you repeat (year after year) patterns that are frustrating to you? Describe the circles.
- Imagine yourself at your worst. How do you use this weak, suffering, helpless self to get your way with other persons? (Do you collect nobility points for constant striving? Martyr points for doing distasteful duty? Poor-little-me points for being sick?)
- Tell about the sorrowful, tragic battles of your soul in a way that will make your audience laugh instead of cry.

Here are some clues to help you reverse your story.

- Sick people are powerful. They make the healthy feel guilty.
- The fears of the weak and fragile establish the limits of any relationship. The meek inherit the earth by sapping the energies of the bold.
- Victims enjoy the luxury of saying, "I can't." When you were young you got punished if you said, "I won't," and helped if you said, "I can't."

Suffering, healing and dying were arts with which traditional cultures equipped every person. The modern medical enterprise is organized to kill pain, eliminate sickness and abolish the need for the art of suffering and dying. Pain is now detached from any context that could give it meaning and turned into a technical problem that has to be solved by the physician . . . in traditional cultures pain was a part of man's participation in a marred universe. Its meaning was cosmic and mythic and not individual and technical.
IVAN ILLICH,
conversation with Sam Keen,
Psychology Today

Someday My Prince Will Come

My visions about my life have always been so grand that any change of direction is a major undertaking. The first big leap I ever made was leaving Europe during the first World War. I was still a young girl, the oldest of five children. Things in Vienna did not look good for us, so I quit my job, took a boat to America, found work, and sent for my brothers and sister. My sister died, but now, fifty years later, the boys are still with me.

I grew up steeped in German romanticism, so naturally I had grand fantasies about passionate love and adventure, finding my prince and walking with him into eternity. But first I had to settle the family and make certain that we would be financially secure. A certain gentleman helped me set up shop here and then took financial advantage of me. I was horribly shocked! How could a nice, elderly man do that to a young girl? After that I was careful never to trust anyone in matters of money.

I taught my brothers to be hairdressers and married a man who gave me security though he was not my prince. We were divorced after thirty years, but in the meantime I bought some property on a hill in California and moved the whole family (the boys and my own two children) up there. All of them expected me to be the Rock of Gibraltar, and I didn't let them down. I was still privately waiting for my Only Beloved, but meanwhile the duties of the blood took priority over longings of the flesh. Year after year I watched over everything. In fact, I played my cards so well that eventually I was virtually invulnerable to outside forces. I've always been broad-minded—all sorts of people pass through my life—but my self-control protected me from contamination. No one could take advantage of me because I stuck to my own affairs; understand what I mean? My family and I were never invaded.

All those years while I plotted a safe course I told myself that this is the way we Jews had to do in order not to be invaded by wrong ideas and materialism and sexual indulgence. The family stayed together (we all still live on this hill), the children stayed close to home, the property tripled in value, the community knew who we were. But when I was sixty I stepped down from my pedestal long enough to see the price I'd paid: my prince had never come. The romantic dream of one-to-one union was dead. Seeking to have and give security had bought me such invulnerability that there was no prince around passionate enough to wake up Snow White. After sixty years I saw that the Rock of Gibraltar was a hunk of stone.

It was a mistake to think that security and passion could exist in the same apple cart. One upsets the other! I hated to let go of that dream, but passion is too ephemeral, too deceptive; everybody knows it burns you out and brings

Suffering is the path of consciousness, and by it living beings arrive at the possession of self-consciousness. For to possess consciousness of oneself, to possess personality, is to know oneself and to feel oneself distinct from other beings, and this feeling of distinction is only reached through an act of collision, through suffering . . . through the sense of one's own limits.
MIGUEL DE UNAMUNO,
Tragic Sense of Life

early death. If you become one of the masses you are lost. And if you are lost, prosperity can't find you. The great passions are a thing of the past, I decided. What I wanted was to rise above romance and fleshly appetites, to be independent, even of God. . . .

So for twelve years I've been endeavoring to recast my romantic dream in spiritual terms, something more appropriate to my age. Now the men I fall in love with are gurus, men with a spiritual fire in their souls to whom I can respond from a distance. Zorba always dies, but the realm of Gurdjieff and Meher Baba lives on eternally. When death comes for you the body disintegrates but the soul survives: there are no limits to one's possibilities after death.

But sometimes I fear that I've gone too far, that I can no more abandon myself to spiritual rapture than I could to romantic passion. . . . I don't know, there's still time, maybe another way will come to me. . . .

The only true wisdom lives far from mankind, out in the great lone-liness, and it can be reached only through suffering. Privation and suffering alone can open the mind of a man to all that is hidden to others.
Eskimo shaman

In fact, just last night I dreamed that as I was stepping into the bathtub a strange woman appeared and said, "Why are you bathing here? The water is full of blood." I said, "But why shouldn't I bathe in it? It's my own blood!" She led me into the living room and pointed to a square, sunken tub in the center of the floor full of clear water. She suggested that I bathe in there. "In front of everybody?" I protested. "All the rest of the family bathes in the bathroom, I've always done it that way, why shouldn't I go on?" When I woke up I felt that maybe the woman was suggesting a new, unstructured path for me. Maybe now I am to come down to the ground where everyone else is, bathe in public, expose myself in front of everyone, become vulnerable—the one thing I've always dreaded. Maybe sinking down is actually the other side of the path to enlightenment! Even talking this way feels like some kind of preparation for death, returning to the earth what belongs to the earth. But if I let go of my controls, I'd run around madly embracing everybody, and then wouldn't I lose my uniqueness, my soul? It's so terribly difficult to know for sure. . . .

Deliver me, Lord, from the sadness at my own suffering which self-love might give, but put into me a sadness like your own.
RENÉ PASCAL

—ESTHER, a grandmother living in San Diego, was born in Vienna of the aristocracy

PLANNING TO BE HUMAN

Plans are dangerous necessities. If we plan too much, we're always living ahead of ourselves, rehearsing scenes that usually don't happen. We can spend a lifetime paying for insurance against catastrophes that never materialize. Those who live in the future miss many of the pleasures of the present. But if we refuse to plan at all, there are some kinds of fulfillment we miss. Many of the most beautiful flowers bloom only when carefully fertilized and cultivated; art involves discipline; learning guitar or gourmet cooking requires an investment of energy over a period of time.

Something in each of us resists making decisions and plans. When the imagination is soaring each decision feels like a forced landing, a little death. But when we act we strengthen our self-definition and gain personal power.

Decisions dealing with self-change may be creative or destructive. A shade too much pressure and our ideals can turn into whiplike demands. Will-power (the revolutionary minority in the psyche) dictates to the entire body how life and personality are to be structured. Heavy-handed dictators provoke repression and rebellion. Won't-power always counters will-power; those aspects of the personality that don't fit into a five-year-ideal-self plan resist the dictates of the will. The result is schizophrenia, civil war.

When there's a gun at your head, it's tough to relax and let change occur. Psychological and political growth toward a more harmonious state usually happens naturally when self-acceptance is high and the pressure for change is gentle. That's when dry decisions can flower into creative choice.

Viewpoints

Keep one eye on what dissatisfies you about yourself now, and it is easier to design a satisfying future. Imagine that you have a fatal disease and have one month left to live.

- What do you still want to do? How will you spend the month of life that remains to you? (Give yourself full energy, plenty of money, and freedom from pain until the end.)
- What will be the epitaph on your tombstone?

Good news—you've just been granted a reprieve. You have a long time to live—ten, twenty, seventy years, who knows. . . . What will you do with your time?

The camel driver has his plans; and the camel has his own plans. The organized mind can think well. The complete man can exist well.
RASUL SHAH

- Draw a floor plan of a house you would like to be living in ten years hence. Who lives with you? What are the physical surroundings like? What is the mood of the place?
- How do you spend your time inside and outside the house? With whom? What is your work?
- What feelings do you experience that were strange to you ten years ago?
- When you have done this fantasy put it aside and do it another way. Give yourself a variety of alternative futures to move around in.

Fantasies are loaded because they put us in touch with our repressed or unrealized desires. Once a desire becomes conscious it demands some kind of response. If we don't say yes or no to specific fantasies, frustration can immobilize us. Move from fantasy to decision. Pick one of the desires uncovered in your exploration of dreams and fantasies and commit yourself to taking the first steps toward its realization. Plan some future action that will positively alter the external or internal world in which you live.

One must assume responsibility for being in a weird world. . . . You must learn to make every act count, since you are going to be here for only a short while, in fact, too short for witnessing all the marvels of it. . . . Let each of your acts be your last battle on earth. Only under those conditions will your acts have their rightful power. Otherwise, they will be . . . the acts of a timid man.
DON JUAN,
Journey to Ixtlan

If I Had a Month to Live I Would:

- Ask my doctor for the name and address of someone who had *two* months to live so that at last I could be relevant to the rest of someone else's life
- Try to talk a record company into buying my guaranteed

Buddy Holly–type interrupted success story (or that of Janis Joplin, Jimi Hendrix, messages beyond the grave . . .)
- Consider hijacking a plane and dropping money over Glastonbury, Connecticut
- Weigh the benefits of political assassination

If I Had a Month to Live I Would:

I have observed that a life directed to an aim is in general better, richer, and healthier than an aimless one, and that it is better to go forward with the stream of time than backwards against it. . . . I am convinced that it is hygienic . . . to discover in death a goal towards which one can strive, and that shrinking away from it is something unhealthy and abnormal which robs the second half of life of its purpose.
C. G. JUNG,
The Portable Jung

- Not tell anyone
- Try to make every moment meaningful
- Pace myself in such a way that I could accomplish more
- Spend more time in spiritual growth
- Pray and meditate more for good karma
- Give away all my personal belongings to people who would need and appreciate them
- Arrange for my own cremation
- Tell all my friends and family how much I love them

If I Had a Month to Live I Would:

- Invite everyone around here to a party
- Give everything I own away to the guests
- Stock up on necessary drugs
- Buy a super high-fidelity tape deck (portable) and a very good motion picture camera with plenty of film
- Arrange for someone to retrieve the full tapes and films after I'm gone

If I Had a Month to Live I Would:

- Make love a lot
- Enjoy my children! Listen beneath their words to the world they live in. Tape record some things I would like to have told them when they were older.
- Eat and talk with friends, and visit my mother, brother, and sisters
- Fly to Paris and spend several days in the most luxurious hotel there and buy expensive presents for all my friends

and charge them to my American Express credit card
(sorry, the deceased left no forwarding address)

- Fly to the most remote South Sea island I could find and
  spend several days with nothing but sun and sea
- Come home and spend my last days among familiar
  things preparing for the unfamiliar thing
- (I would like *not* to write a little book on the last month
  of life, though I probably would)

If I Had a Month to Live I Would:

- Go on working, as always

—VARIOUS CONTRIBUTORS

*The Future. Planting
trees early in spring,
we make a place for
birds to sing
in time to come. How
do we know?
They are singing here
now
There is no other guar-
antee
that singing will ever be*
WENDELL BERRY,
A Part

6

COSMIC TIME

Transcending Here and Now

The dates on the tombstone—John Doe 1937–2009—mark the outer limits of a single life; seventy-two years in Illinois. That's all there is for John.

Or is it? Sometimes a crack opens in time and we wonder whether there are other ways of timing and spacing our lives:

The dream was especially vivid. I knew someone had drowned while skin diving and I had to search for the body. I put on an aqualung and went to the bottom of the narrow channel of water. I found nothing. Suddenly I was swept away by a current. I knew I would be drowned. But I wasn't. In the next scene I was explaining to the military officer in charge of the search for the body how I had miraculously escaped death. . . . I was so shaken by the dream I got up and wrote it down. Five or six hours later I received news that a close friend of mine just drowned while skin diving off the coast of Maine.

If mind is encapsulated in body, how can it travel in time and space?

There are enough accounts of clairvoyance, ESP, and mystical awareness to make any reasonable person question the dogma that says we are all complete captives of clock time and geographical space. The question is not whether we can transcend sequential time but in what ways we do so. Religious persons speak of atemporal experiences as vistas opening to God, Spirit, Universal Mind, the Void, or the Cosmos. Others consider them subjective states of mind, an "oceanic feeling" (Freud), or a state of psychedelic awareness.

We are in the middle of a consciousness revolution in which orthodox religion and traditional science are being overthrown. For many people God is truly dead. The formal practices of religion do not, for many people, produce transcendence. There is also a weariness with the closed push-pull universe of popular science. Widespread experimentation with techniques for transcendence (drugs, meditation, yoga, divination, astrology, prayer, ritual, dance) reflects our desire to recapture a magical sense of the openness of the cosmos. We want out of the impersonal, anonymous universe where everything can be explained by the laws of cause and effect and probability. We long to regain the primitive feeling that nature (Gaia) has some kindly, even motherly intent toward her human creations. And why deny that some force at least as intelligent as an Apple computer (and perhaps more tender) might be responsible for morning glories and the insatiable human appetite for significance?

A free person is a cognitive outlaw, one who rejects official ideologies and interprets experience with homemade categories. In considering what journeys may be taken in and out of ordinary time it helps to stick close to raw experience and avoid the packaged explanations and language of religion, psychology, or science.

THE TWO-FACED WORLD

It seems as if the world was designed, or not designed, to drive us mad. We think we recognize order but then chaos makes it all absurd. Reality is schizophrenic; order and accident, design and chance are locked in eternal battle.

Most of the time the universe appears to be gov-

*The great sea
Has sent me adrift,
It moves me as the weed
in a great river,
Earth and the great
weather move me,
Have carried me away,
And move my inward
parts with joy.*
ESKIMO WOMAN SHAMAN, as quoted by RASMUSSEN in *News of the Universe* by Robert Bly

The real problem is that we are used to looking at the world simply. We are accustomed to believing that something is there or it is not there. Whether we look at it or not, it is either there or it is not there. Our experience tells us that the physical world is solid, real, and independent of us. Quantum mechanics says, simply, that this is not so.
GARY ZUKAV, *The Dancing Wu Li Masters*

In the very earliest time, when both people and animals lived on earth, a person could become an animal if he wanted to and an animal could become a human being. Sometimes they were people and sometimes animals and there was no difference. All spoke the same language. That was the time when words were like magic. The human mind had mysterious powers. A word spoken by chance might have strange consequences. It would suddenly come alive and what people wanted to happen could happen— all you had to do was say it. Nobody can explain this: That's the way it was.

After Nalungiaq (Eskimo), *"Magic Words"*

I shall never believe that God plays dice with the world.

ALBERT EINSTEIN

erned by rational powers. Things usually happen according to the rules. The tides follow mathematically calculable patterns. Acorns regularly grow into oak trees, not persimmons. When we see the starry skies above we secretly suspect (as Immanuel Kant argued) that some provident God designed the world. Things seem to fit together (men and women). Causes and effects were made for each other. The evidence suggests (*almost* beyond reasonable doubt) that reason governs reality.

Most cultures have assumed that some divine mind or minds are homogenized with nature and that it's possible to harmonize human life with the will of God, with the Tao, with the force that draws the pine trees toward the sun, with the laws of nature. The Greeks contemplated the stars and thought they could pattern their politics and ethics on the divine regularities that ruled the heavens. With less reverence but equal hope we use space probes and computers to track down the hidden logic in things. And we trust that one day our sacred science will dispel the mystery and reveal the predictable order that lies beneath apparent chance.

But just when we are about to pronounce the universe sane it shows its other face. We expect the usual thing to happen and along comes a snowstorm in August, a deformed child, or a duck-billed platypus. Chance and accident seem to be stronger than law and order. And, worst of all, the wrong people die young. There is no moral or logical reason why a child should die of leukemia. When some misfit makes an impossible shot and kills our President, it's hard to escape the impression that some indifferent God is playing bingo with the universe.

The arbitrariness of things is enough to give anyone who thinks about it a case of existential anxiety or a taste for superstition and magical rituals. Lady Luck's a fickle bitch and it's hard to figure out how she operates, yet some people definitely have the knack for walking out of accidents and picking horses. Maybe luck is nothing more than being open to whatever happens and avoiding the illusion that reason rules. Lucky people know the world is magical so they're not surprised by accidents; like children and drunks, they relax when they fall. And who is to say that magic is irrational? If everything is disjointed a black cat may be more predictive of the future than computerized trends. Why not cut the deck, or read Tarot cards, or consult fortune cookies? Maybe these are precisely the liturgies that win the favor of Lady Luck.

It is no wonder that many of us are a little confused. To survive in the world we have to learn how and when to use reason or intuition, investigation or divination, logic or magic. At best, there is never enough order in things to satisfy our appetite for harmony. But neither is chaos sufficiently consistent to destroy our fascination with reason. After you've done everything else you can think of, it never hurts to cross your fingers.

I say that we are wound With mercy round and round As if with air.
GERARD MANLEY HOPKINS

Viewpoints

Religion has been used as a tuning fork to adjust the vibrations of an individual life to the rhythms of the cosmos. Whether we use meditation, dice, prayer, daisy petals, or astrology, each of us has some way of keeping in touch with the governing rhythms of the world.

- How do you stay together with the basic rhythms of your psyche and nature?
- What cycles do you experience in your body that are responsive to the moon or the seasons?
- What do you do when you are out of sync, when everything's going wrong, when you get up on the wrong side of the bed, when you can't get it together?

Although we can't defend our superstitions rationally, most of us practice some magical rituals to court good luck and ward off evil.

The true purpose of all spiritual disciplines is to clear away whatever may block our awareness of that which is God in us. The aim is to get rid of whatever may so distract the mind and encumber the life that we function without this awareness.
HOWARD THURMAN, *Disciplines of the Spirit*

- What lucky objects protect you against the irrationality of the world? (A crystal or stone, four-leaf clover, St. Christopher medal, a favorite shirt?) Do you depend on them? What would you do if you lost one of them?
- When you have to make decisions and the alternatives seem evenly balanced, what do you do? (Flip a coin and do the opposite, cast the I Ching, visit your psychiatrist, pray, consult the stars?)
- What rituals do you have for warding off bad luck? (Crossing yourself, knocking on wood, avoiding ladders and stepping over cracks, throwing salt over your shoulder?)

The Old Oak

Eden is. The kingdom of the Father is spread upon the earth, and men do not see it.
JOSEPH CAMPBELL,
The Power of Myth

When I lose my path I have certain ways of finding it again. Sometimes I take a large sheet of paper and make a list of beautiful scenes. They always have to do with my childhood: something about the ocean, or dark Florida nights when the stars hang down so you feel you can reach up and pluck them.

When I turn to my oak tree I'm desperate. It's a huge creature, standing eternally in the back yard of the house where I was born and grew up. In the fall of the year when the storms came up from the Caribbean I would stand at the window of the house watching and listening to the limbs of the peach trees and the persimmons and sometimes the big bay trees snapping under the wind. And then I'd watch the oak tree, and the only thing it did was sway ever so slightly all in one piece, not even dropping a leaf.

So the oak tree and I reached an understanding. As a child, when I had problems I couldn't handle (the kind when you envision yourself in your coffin, and the weeping mother at the graveside, and how sorry they all are that they've done this thing to you), I would think of my tree. No matter what my problem was, if I could get to my oak tree and sit down and lean against it and feel it on my back, then I knew that I could tell my whole sadness and be contained. I worked out all my religious problems under that oak tree. When I couldn't understand what they were saying in church about Jesus, I would sit down there and talk it all out. The oak and Jesus became all mixed up together. I felt such a personal companionship with them that I never had any theological problem about Jesus as the Son of God. It's the same way for me now. Anytime I feel sad or at a loss, I beat a path, in my mind, back to the old oak.

—HOWARD THURMAN is a black Christian mystic, grandson of a slave

Like the Time I Filled a Bag with Apples and Climbed on a Horse to Ride Off Forever

One morning I got up with the sun and felt one of those brilliant crystal days coming on. So my friend David and I threw together some apples and almonds and cider and whizzed through the city to get to the country.

David's place was a Quonset hut in the middle of nowhere with cottonwood trees out front, a couple of horses standing around, an old windmill, and a half-finished geodesic dome. We walked around, visiting the windmill and listening to it squeak, talking to the horses, climbing the dome. After a while I took off all my clothes (except for my boots), tied them around me, and walked off across the hills.

It was a relief to be off the highway, out where you could see things from 360 degrees. I was clumping through the bushes, feeling the depth of things, my feet contacting the earth step by step, entranced by the glitter in the rocks, nothing on my mind except my movement. I was following a cowpath along a fence line and eventually found myself making a large circle. I could hear the horses nickering and tromping around, and I wanted to ride.

One of the horses was an old brood mare with a strange look in her eye; the other one was very young. I wondered if he was her colt, but when I went up and spoke to him I realized that the two of them were simply friends and it would be all right to ride him. Right away I looked around for a rope to fix a bridle but I couldn't find a thing. I kept stumbling over wires and cans and started feeling frustrated. Finally I decided to use a piece of soft wire, but as I was

This that is beautiful, it shows my way; this that is beautiful, it shows my way; this that is beautiful, it shows my way; before me, it is beautiful, it shows my way; behind me it is beautiful, it shows my way; this that is beautiful, it shows my way.
Navajo creation chant

yanking it down from the tin roof I tripped over the perfect piece of rope, curled neatly at my feet. The pleasant surprise rocked me back into slow motion. I put the wire back where it came from and fitted a bridle to the horse.

Then I went to the truck, took out a white paper bag, and started filling it with apples. As I was doing this I got the idea that I was packing for a little longer trip than just across the fields and back, and the fantasy grew in a great rush: I would just go away, leaving the angular part of the world far behind me! As I filled up the bag I felt tremendously excited, thinking about the canyons and sunlight and mist, and me riding off forever.

So I got on the horse, all set to go with a jug in one hand and a bag of apples in the other, and then the horse swung his head around and bit a hole in the bottom of my bag! Everything fell out, apples bumping all over the roadway. I just sat there for a moment. Then I got down and started gathering while the horse munched away on a bright red apple.

The horse bit a hole in my flight plans and brought me to earth in one big bump. He was telling me: not so fast, riding off forever throws everything off balance, this is as far as you have to go today! I climbed back on to see where he was going and we traveled about twenty feet before he stopped cold. I got off, put the rope down, and walked back, laughing at the wonder of it all.

That was a day! Everything fit together in such a perfect circle: speeding along the freeway to get away, feeling the organic beauty of the countryside; getting tangled in the wires of my big plans; the ideal rope appearing at my feet; deciding to ride off forever; the horse showing me I wasn't ready; and then that cascade of bouncing apples. . . . In the silence I could see the folly of trying to force my trip on natural rhythms, trying to blend into the mist and evaporate. The nice thing was that I also recognized the beauty of the true images: the earth, my feet, the sun, the horse, a bag of apples. Everything was there for me. All I had to do was respond.

—JESS is a country girl living in the city,
looking for adventure

Elected Silence, sing to
me
And beat upon my
whorled ear,
Pipe me to pastures still
and be
The music that I care to
hear.
GERARD MANLEY
HOPKINS

MIRACLES, MAGIC, AND SYNCHRONICITY

"I hadn't seen Jane for years but her occasional letters were filled with echoes of darkness. I thought about her often. So when I was in California on business I planned to visit her, but I didn't call ahead of time. The day before I returned home I was driving through the town where she lived and stopped at a roadside phone booth to call her. There was no answer. I left the booth and walked to a nearby gas station to use the men's room. And there was Jane with a flat tire. A coincidence? What does that mean? Though we didn't know what to name the forces that brought us together, we both knew the meeting had been arranged."

Whether the world is intimate or impersonal, lawful or magical depends on your perspective. World views are like glasses: they can be steel gray, rosy, or black and white. In the matter of cosmic sight we all wear some kind of lenses.

Children and primitive peoples live in a personalized universe. They experience events as tailor-made to match their needs. Omens, signs, and miracles flash forth from every tree and hilltop: bushes burn and are not consumed; birds bring messages from the gods; among the Bushmen of Africa, the stars (kinfolk of an earlier race now dwelling in the sky) guide the aim of the hunter; the Hopi snake dance brings summer rains. In childhood we all live at the enchanted center of things. We know that chairs trip us when we're angry; we move through the forest and the thicket opens automatically. The world is a conspiracy contrived to delight us.

But once we become mature we put away childish notions of magic, abandon the egocentric perspective, and learn to observe the world with neutral eyes. We are encouraged to filter out the voices that address us in the wind and rain, close off supernatural whisperings in dreams, and become citizens of a universe that is unresponsive to intuitions. We adopt a skepticism that

Synchronicity designated the parallelism of time and meaning between psychic and psychophysical events, which scientific knowledge so far has been unable to reduce to a common principle. The term explains nothing, it simply formulates the occurrence of meaningful coincidences which, in themselves, are chance happenings, but are so improbable that we must assume them to be based on some kind of principle, or on some property of the empirical world. . . . From this it follows either that the psyche cannot be localized in space, or that space is relative to the psyche.
C. G. JUNG,
The Portable Jung

*Each of us is encased in
an armour whose task is
to ward off signs. Signs
happen to us without
respite, living means be-
ing addressed, we would
need only to present our-
selves and to perceive.
But the risk is too dan-
gerous, the soundless
thunderings seem to
threaten us with annihi-
lation, and from genera-
tion to generation we
perfect the defense appa-
ratus. All our knowl-
edge assures us, "Be
calm, everything hap-
pens as it must happen,
but nothing is directed
at you, you are not
meant; it is just 'the
world,' you can experi-
ence it as you like. . . ."
What occurs to me ad-
dresses me.*
MARTIN BUBER,
Between Man and Man

*All things and all men,
so to speak, call on us
with small or loud voic-
es. They want us to lis-
ten, they want us to un-
derstand their intrinsic
claims, their justice of
being. . . . But we can
give it to them only
through the love that
listens.*
PAUL TILLICH,
Love, Power and Justice

becomes the foundation of what we narrowly identify as reason.

Fortunately, our sophistication does not prevent the world from going its magical way. Things keep happening that jolt our minds; events bend themselves to fit our private needs; hunches pan out; clairvoyant moments burst into daylight consciousness; prophetic dreams visit us in spite of our skepticism; happy accidents, coincidences, or synchronicities are as common as breath.

Viewpoints

Our psyches have an automatic mechanism for shaking off weird experiences which disturb our normal ways of understanding. For years mainstream scientists have been reluctant to admit the existence of UFOs, extra-sensory perception or clairvoyance because they couldn't explain them. Sort through your experiences and bring out the bizarre, marvelous, and inexplicable.

- What fortunate accidents, coincidences, synchro-nicities, or lucky breaks have befallen you?
- What events seem prearranged?
- What premonitions have you had of future events? (Prophetic dreams? Hunches?)
- Describe trances or communications from other people you have received. From the dead?
- What evidence could you collect to support the hypothesis that you are at the center of a world which was planned for you and is responsive to you?

Dear St. Anthony

My life is studded with miracles, like two-cent rhine-stones. I stay in circulation so magic has lots of chances to find me. As a kid I walked around crossing myself and chanting: "Something's lost and can't be found, dear St. Anthony, look around." And I found things: money, medallions, caps, comic books, old photos, everything! One afternoon last month I showed up in San Francisco and went to Lilac Street where an old friend of mine was staying. I didn't know her house number so I walked up and down the four blocks of Lilac until I found the house that felt right—a big Victorian thing with lots of units and porches and clotheslines. I went upstairs and knocked on number 7. Nancy opened the door with a kid in her arms. She was at a neighbor's house baby-sitting for a couple of hours, and she was amazed to see me. . . .

I love pictures. I also like to drop spare change into potluck machines looking for omens. One day I fed a machine at the beach arcade and won some playing cards with pictures of Hollywood cowboys painted on them: Gene Autry, king of diamonds; Roy Rogers, jack of hearts; Fred MacMurray, ten of spades. I put them in my pocket and carried them around with me. A few days later a friend of mine was in a funk and I said, "Here, Alec, I have something for you," and handed him the Fred MacMurray card. It worked like a charm; it spun his head around: it turns out that thirty years ago Fred MacMurray was his Boy Scout master!

Magic or divination or synchronicity is simply making connection with real chemical/electrical bonds of some sort that aren't picked up if you're moving too fast or not looking out for them. The night my father died in Central Islip Mental Hospital four out of his six kids received messages from him. He died between two and four in the morning. Mary, asleep in a ski lodge in Vermont, had a nightmare in which her husband chopped Pop to death with an ax. Kay, who sleeps like Rip Van Winkle, woke unexplainably at two and couldn't get back to sleep for several hours. I was at home getting high with some friends when suddenly, about 1 A.M., I fell into an airless despair. It was so complete that I didn't even try to understand but lay down on the floor and floated in it. At about two it lifted off as fast as it came, so I got up and went right back to talking. My

Eskimo Vision Event I: Go to a lonely place and rub a stone in a circle on a rock for hours and days on end.

Sioux Vision Event III: Go to a mountain-top and cry for a vision.
JEROME ROTHENBERG,
Shaking the Pumpkin

The Bushman . . . lived in an extraordinary intimacy with nature. . . . Wherever he went . . . he felt that he was known. We are a generation of know-alls. But few of us have the life-giving feeling of being known. Wherever this little man went he was known. The trees knew him; the animals knew him as he knew them; the stars knew him. His sense of relationship was so vivid that he could speak of "our brother the Vulture." He looked up at the stars and he spoke of "Grandmother Sirius," of "Grandfather Canis" because this was the highest title of honor which he could bestow.
LAURENS VAN DER POST,
Patterns of Renewal

sister called the next morning to say the old man was dead. My brother showed up soon after, and when I told him he said, "I knew it! I woke Pamela up in the night to tell her the old man croaked in my dream!" Our father was a madman, but his madness was rooted in common magic: his death was electric with it.

—JOE is an Irish-American actor,
playwright, and gambler

Here Is There and Then Is Now

Ten years ago I was convinced that there was nothing psychic about me. But as I went deeper into yoga and meditation and Edgar Cayce's books I began to wonder.

One day I went with a friend to a class in psychic development and ended up enrolling. The teacher was a medium who would sometimes fall into trances and strange voices would speak through her, a thing which later happened to a few other members of the class. It was there that I first heard of psychometry. The teacher explained that people leave vibrations on objects that they own or hold for any length of time, and a sensitive is often able to know things about the person's past lives by holding the item and concentrating. At first I didn't like psychometry, I didn't see how I could possibly distinguish between the fantasies of my own vivid imagination and a true reading. Then one day I was meditating at a Quaker meeting and feeling deeply peaceful when quite unexpectedly I experienced myself as somebody else. I was sitting there dressed in long dark clothes surrounded by four children, obviously mine. There was a bonnet on my head and I knew my name, Hannah, Hannah Whitfield or Whitcomb—I wasn't quite sure. At that moment I was engulfed by a deep, anguished feeling of bereavement. I knew that my husband had just been buried; he'd been chopping wood and the ax had glanced off a knot in the log and gone into his left leg, causing death by infection. I sat promising myself and his memory that somehow I'd bring up our children properly by myself.

It all happened in a flash. Even as I was saying to myself,

Last night I asked the moon about the Moon, my one question for the visible world, Where is God? The moon says: I am dust stirred up when he passed by. The sun: My face is pale yellow from just now seeing him. Water: I slide on my head and face like a snake, from a spell he said. Fire: His lightning, I want to be that restless. Wind, why so light?: I would burn if I had a choice. Earth, quiet and thoughtful?: Inside me I have a garden and an underground spring.
RUMI,
Open Secret

"Wow, what an imagination!" I somehow knew it was nothing of the sort. My imagination just isn't that good, so many details, so fast, so undirected. Could I have tuned into some earlier life?

Nothing else like that happened for a few months until I began giving yoga lessons to my friend Lee at her house in the country. Lee is one of the most psychic people I've ever known. The two of us started playing with the Ouija board and we began to get interesting messages from the other side. Soon her friend Ed joined us. We sat at the board every week, and my life took on a new excitement that hasn't left it since. We began to see bits and pieces of our past lives fitting together. In one of them I was married to Ed, and a slender handsome man named Ernst was my lover. One day Ernst spoke through the board, asking to be my spiritual guide. When I accepted (a bit dubiously) the pointer looped and figure-eighted all over the board with his rejoicing, and my life was changed forever.

After that, other visions from past lives would pop into my mind when I meditated. It was quite unlike ordinary thinking; more like when you've been trying hard to remember a name and as soon as you give up it pops bright and clear into your mind. Often these memories come flooded with associated emotion. For instance, I remember one day emerging from meditation sobbing over the vision of Ernst being gored to death by a bull that had surprised us while we were making love in a field in sixteenth-century Belgium.

As my psychic life opened up, my gift for psychometry grew too, and I worked with other people more and more. Holding an object between my palms, I would sit quietly with my eyes closed and my mind as still as I could hold it. I'd give a silent prayer for protection and guidance and turn inward for the other person. I was astonished at the variety of pictures that unfolded, sometimes in considerable detail. I found that if I asked a question silently such as, "What country?" or "What century?" I would somehow usually know the answer. I could work only a short time, however, before the pictures became dim or I started feeling my imagination taking over and had to stop. If I was very tired nothing happened at all.

The Pygmies have been in the forest for many thousands of years. It is their world. . . . They know the tiny sounds that tell where the bees have hidden their honey; they recognize the kind of weather that brings a multitude of different mushrooms springing to the surface. . . . The exact moment when termites swarm, at which they must be caught to provide an important delicacy, is a mystery to any but the people of the forest. They know the secret language that is denied all outsiders and without which life in the forest is an impossibility.
COLIN TURNBULL,
The Forest People

Ideas come from space.
THOMAS EDISON

This we know. The earth does not belong to man; man belongs to the earth. Whatever befalls the earth befalls the sons of earth. This we know. All things are connected like the blood which unites one family. All things are connected.
CHIEF SEATTLE

The center is every-where.
FRIEDRICH NIETZSCHE

Early on I looked into the lives of a particularly gentle girl and saw her as a Scythian chieftain, returning to the battlefield after a battle with the Greeks. He was searching for his young son who had gone into battle by his side. I hesitated there, as I didn't know who the Scythians were or if they'd ever fought the Greeks (later research proved that they had), but the scene led me on. I watched the chieftain heaving aside several bloody corpses and uncovering the mutilated body of his son. I don't know if I shared his revulsion or whether it was just my own I was feeling, but I felt such a wave of nausea that I nearly gagged, throwing the ring back at its owner. It was ten minutes before I was normal again. I realized that the warrior's soul lesson had been so violent that this gentle person had never again returned in a male body.

Another time I saw a girl as a native woman in Brazil. She had carelessly left her young child playing by the river and she and I watched in helpless horror as the great jaws of a crocodile closed on one round leg and dragged him screaming under water. I handed back her article, saying I believed that the little boy had returned in this life as her three-year-old son. She stared at me in wonder. "You couldn't have known," she said, "but lately he's been afraid of the dark. He has the idea that there's a crocodile in his room trying to eat him up!"

I was as awed as she was. It's very hard to shake the suspicion that you're making everything up out of whole cloth. Again and again I've had verification, and yet I'm always surprised because I always suspect myself. Every time I begin a reading I explain to the person that I have no idea if what I recount is the truth or not, that they alone can know, because it is their soul memory that I'm trying to pipe into, and the knowledge is buried in their subconscious.

Ernst, my guide from the other world, explained to us that we're working with a natural energy which is as real as electricity or television. "Actually, it's more like radio than anything else," he told us. "Some days you can get a far-off station clearly and yet another day the same tuning gives you nothing but gobbledygook. Someday the scientific world will recognize psychometry and be able to control it as they do radio."

I wonder what will happen next! Now I'm much more available and vulnerable to good and evil powers than most people are. But I'm not afraid, I'm "on the path," so my life is filled with joy and purpose.

—MITZI is the daughter of Esther ("Someday My Prince Will Come"), a Quaker and practicing psychometrist

PARADISE: LOST AND FOUND

Once upon a time we were all natives of paradise. Some say it was a garden of delight; some say it was a gold-paved city luminous with justice and good will. At the very least it was a state of unbroken pleasure.

But something happened. The serpent entered; paradise vanished; primeval childhood ended; ego ate id; the bourgeoisie gained control of the means of production and exploited the working class; separation anxiety led us to possess the world and make it safe by work; the pain of parental rejection numbed our nerve endings and our wonder.

It is widely agreed that alienation is the condition of man but there is no agreement about how he fell from grace. From a psychological point of view the process is easily described. Early in the socialization process a child learns that she can get love only if she denies desire and obeys parents and other big people. Thus she develops a split—a polite schizophrenia for nice people—between private feeling and public action. The child learns—is taught—to be a double agent. Her private world is a paradise where the pleasure principle governs; to survive she becomes a naturalized citizen of the adult world governed by the reality principle. Every child knows when she consents to citizenship in the real world that she is betraying paradise. In time she adjusts; only infrequently do remembrances of childhood happiness trouble her righteousness.

But periodic pleasure creates a hunger for more. Some fools and some heroes insist that if paradise has been lost it can be regained. Wise men warn us that

To find your own way is to follow your own bliss. This involves analysis, watching yourself and seeing where the real deep bliss is—not the quick little excitement, but the real, deep, life-filling bliss.
JOSEPH CAMPBELL

Hope is a memory of the future.
GABRIEL MARCEL

The wolf also shall dwell with the lamb, and the leopard shall lie down with the kid; . . . and a little child shall lead them . . . They shall not hurt nor destroy in all my holy mountain: for the earth shall be full of the knowledge of the Lord, as the waters cover the sea.
Isaiah

this may be an illusion. They counsel us to accept the necessity of alienation: better to settle for civilization and its discontents than to dream of paradise and wake up cold, hungry, afraid, angry, lost, and disillusioned. Freud told us: work and love; the world is too dangerous for children.

Whether or not we can ever create a society of the unalienated, we can at least lessen the alienation in ourselves. Every person has traces of paradise inside. If we once locate our feelings of harmony we can learn to move in and out of them almost at will. Memories of primal pleasure are alive and well in the unconscious; all we need to do is call them forth.

In analysis the small and lonely child that is hidden behind his achievements wakes up and asks: "What would have happened if I had appeared before you, bad, ugly, angry, jealous, lazy, dirty, smelly? Where would your love have been then? And I was all these things as well. Does this mean that it was not really me whom you loved, but only what I pretended to be? . . . What became of my childhood? Have I not been cheated out of it? I can never return to it. I can never make up for it. From the beginning I have been a little adult.
ALICE MILLER,
The Drama of the Gifted Child

Viewpoints

To remember the fall is to move a step closer to paradise. Beneath primal pain lies primal pleasure; we only hate those we loved; the apple was even more delicious before it became a forbidden fruit.

- When did you fall from grace, lose your ease?
- When do you first remember lying? Being ashamed? Hiding? Feeling small and inadequate? When did you get your second face?
- When did you discover the limitations in your mother? Best friend? A hero?

Allow your thoughts to float back to the most ecstatic times of childhood. Remember how your body felt when you could run tirelessly, when there was no tomorrow or yesterday, when everything in the world was just right, when you felt loved and secure and free. Try to recapture specific scenes.

- What keeps you out of the garden now?
- A hypothesis: the hard realism of adult consciousness is abnormal and the childhood state of appreciation is the natural state of awareness. Now what?

Solitary Confinement

I don't know exactly how I fell from grace, but I definitely knew when I was down. Thud. It had something to do with slipping out of my mother's lap when she would gladly have rocked me and held me longer: I was three years old and had no time for baby stuff. I was too busy rushing after my older sister and brother, hustling to keep them from noticing that I had a little trouble walking, running, climbing, spelling, and reading at their speed. More than comfort, I wanted the big time.

So, suddenly I wasn't a child anymore but a small double agent, consciously conning a world that wasn't mine. Since I was my only confidant I would plan and scheme and talk to myself when I was alone. My fall from innocence was literal. I bit into consciousness and then *it* began to eat *me*.

I started collecting things, hoarding. Boxes of banana popsicles hidden in the basement freezer under loaves of Wonder Bread. My diary full of petty confessions. And money. I remember those horrid, breezeless summer afternoons when I'd close myself in my room, dig my alligator-skin squeeze-purse out of my rainboots, pour the coins on the bed, and start counting. Oh, it was a miserable ritual! With the door bolted no one ever interrupted me, but at the same time I was trapped in there. My careful private accounting system kept me safe and captive.

Now I try to avoid that airless six-year-old's room whenever I have the choice. It feels like a death trap. I try to stay outside, keep moving, visit friends on their turf, but sometimes I fall into states of mind that have the same sticky, suffocating feeling of that other room, and then, instantly, I am a prisoner. Since I don't trust anyone to come in there with me (aren't two immobilized twice as miserable as one?) I go in there utterly alone, resigned to do my time as intensely as I can to get it over with. Sometimes I manage to dig my way out, but otherwise I only hope to finish out my sentence.

The paradise of preambivalent harmony, for which so many patients hope, is unattainable. But the experience of one's own truth . . . makes it possible to return to one's own world of feelings at an adult level—without paradise, but with the ability to mourn.
ALICE MILLER,
The Drama of the Gifted Child

—PHYLLIS is a poet, the middle child in
a large family in middle America

GOOD AND EVIL—AND BEYOND

Go(o)d and (D)evil depend on each other like concave and convex. The same instinct in us that personifies good into God transforms evil into Devil. We put human faces on good and evil to try to humanize the universe. God created man in His image and man returned the favor. One of the reasons we create gods and angels is because we want to believe that the world is ruled by benevolent powers. But when these powers do not eliminate suffering, tragedy, and death, we evoke a panoply of devils, "walk-ins," and monsters to absorb the blame for evil.

Because gods and goddesses do not die they reassure us that something abides; beyond our time and space there is a reality invulnerable to death; the Rock of Ages is not washed away by the river. The logic of religion is reflected in the primitive practice of driving an *axis mundi*—a world-pole—into the ground at the place where a mystic, shaman, or priest has received a vision or revelation of God. The tribe, then, organizes its life around this point—the sacred center of the world. All lines radiate from the church steeple (or the Capitol building); the holy is the centering point for human life, the firm foundation, the Eternal Rock. Paul Tillich translated this religious act into psychological language when he said that whatever concerns us ultimately is our God. Even if "God is dead" the presence of the holy permeates the place where our needs for security and meaning are met. Whatever passion is at the center of our lives—work, money, family, music, education, politics, romance—promises salvation and demands ultimate loyalty.

The Devil is still with us. The forces of evil are organized and, consciously or unconsciously, they conspire against us. They are out to get us: The Russians, Khadafi, the Ayatollah, computer viruses, yuppie bankers, the Pentagon, drug cartels, cancer, AIDS, the Mafia, Big Brother. Or (for psychological sophisticates who don't believe in projection or the

There is no doubt that healthy-mindedness is inadequate as a philosophical doctrine, because the evil facts which it positively refuses to account for are a genuine portion of reality; and they may after all be the best key to life's significance, and possibly the only openers of our eyes to the deepest levels of truth.
WILLIAM JAMES,
Varieties of Religious Experience

Devil) evil is reduced to abstract qualities within the self: fear, hostility, passivity, repression, primal pain, or weak will.

Regardless of what we call them, our modern dualisms divide us as much as the old ones did: whether we project Good and Evil outward on God and the Devil or inward on Eros and Aggression the split remains. And a split world means a perpetual battleground between the white and the black, a habitat for schizophrenics. The effort to root out the evil we create by our definitions spreads the disease. In the long run our best solution is to proclaim an armistice, an end to dualism, and welcome the warring factions into the human commonwealth. The opposites belong together, the contradictions can be encompassed. The Devil is Lucifer, God's fallen angel; Eros waits under Aggression; strength is hidden just below the fault in personality. An old Eastern proverb sums it up: "Where you stumble and fall there you will find the gold." Nietzsche pointed the way toward the unity of personality when he challenged us to go "beyond good and evil." We can trust life to break through our brittle moral judgments and rise up like a seedling from the husks of its old confines.

You yourself are participating in the evil, or you are not alive. Whatever you do is evil for somebody. This is one of the ironies of the whole creation.
JOSEPH CAMPBELL,
The Power of Myth

Viewpoints

Even if we have no official organizational chart we all have a private demonology. (To whom does your Secretary of Greed report? Do you have separate ministries for the Seven Deadly Sins?) What demons, devils, ghouls, witches, evil spirits, monsters (or shadows, frustrations, fears, inhibitions, repressions, and complexes) make up your private underworld?

I do not understand my own actions. For I do not do what I want, but I do the very thing I hate.
SAINT PAUL,
Romans

- How is your hell organized? Draw a map, make a chart, or compile a catalogue of personnel.
- As Commander-in-Chief of the Forces of Light, how do you combat the Powers of Darkness? What evil do you wage war against? How?

We are faced with evil. And, as for me, I feel rather as Augustine did before becoming a Christian where he said: "I tried to find the source of evil and I got nowhere." But it is also true that I, and a few others, know what must be done, if not to reduce evil, at least not to add to it. Perhaps we cannot prevent this world from being a world in which children are tortured. But we can reduce the number of tortured children.
ALBERT CAMUS,
Resistance, Rebellion and Death

- As the Prince of Darkness, how do you undermine the Forces of Light?
- The bad guys should get what's coming to them. In your hell how are offenders punished? What is the appropriate punishment? Reward?

If this were the best of all possible worlds we might love mystery more and explanations less. But since evil shatters our security we tell stories to explain why a world that is so intricate and marvelous is invariably shadowed by tragedy. All people create a myth to explain why evil exists: because Satan rebelled against God, or because spirit and matter are incompatible, or because the cosmic consciousness is not yet fully awakened, or because the bourgeoisie exploits the proletariat, or . . .

- Make up your own myth. Why are pain and malevolence in the world? Is there an end to evil?

The Greeks personified their ultimate concerns by creating a pantheon of gods and goddesses: Aphrodite, goddess of love; Pan, god of wild things; Athena, goddess of the polis; Zeus, ruler of Olympus . . . Describe the pantheon of the gods that move you. Give names and faces to the concerns at the center of your life.

The Leer of the Monkey Devil

A few years back I woke up in the middle of the night filled with a vast terror. I hadn't been dreaming and couldn't explain my sudden fright, except that I sensed the presence of evil in the room. I began to stare at the upper left-hand corner above my bed and I saw a creature slowly take shape like a storm cloud. It was a monkey, black but glowing around the edges, with venom and filth and slime drooling down his hairy face. He just hung there dribbling and cackling and all the time his phosphorescent eyes were riveted on me. I lay on my back trembling and whimpering.

My bones were like water. He hovered there, waiting, his menacing arms waving like poisonous tentacles. I knew that he was concentrated evil, and that all of his emanations were directed at me.

I'm a firm rationalist, but the existence of this thing was never disputable. This wasn't a nightmare or fantasy projection; it was an actual demon filling me with supernatural energy. I tore my mind apart searching for the reason why he was here, but there was no answer. He simply was. My mind was infected as well as my body; there was no escape from his pervasive evil. Finally I got hold of myself enough to say: "Okay, he's here and he's got me, so *what's going to happen?*" And I thought: *He's going to kill me.* Then I remembered that car accidents and falling rocks lead to the same thing, and that death would at least put a stop to this torture. Slowly, slowly, the monkey began to fade and the evil began to neutralize. I ran my hands over my body and found that I was still there. And then he was gone.

Caged monkeys always strike me as degraded animals; slimy and servile and vindictive, all day long imitating humans like mirrors in a madhouse. That's how my monkey was, spewing ugly reflections of myself through his crazy leer. But his appearance marked the first time in my life that I wasn't able to draw a moral from an experience, the first time I accepted the fantastic without any rationale. So now I have a strange feeling of friendliness toward him, a little as if he was a gift from the gods, or a minor foot soldier detached from the army of the Devil to bring me a taste of absolute terror. That monkey devil is permanently seated in my reality. I don't actually think about him much, but I know that sooner or later (what kind of a schedule could he be on?) he'll be back to give me another dose. Wherever he is and whatever evil he embodies, he clearly belongs to me.

—ISAAC is an architect and a Vietnam veteran

A Time and a Place for Everything

My world is full of gods and goddesses, but they aren't the kind that sit on Mount Olympus. They stir among

Man aggresses not only out of frustration and fear but out of joy, plenitude, love of life. Men kill lavishly out of the sublime joy of heroic triumph over evil. . . . Most men will not usually kill unless it is under the banner of some kind of fight against evil. . . . I think it is time for social scientists to catch up with Hitler as a psychologist, and to realize that men will do anything for heroic belonging to a victorious cause if they are persuaded about the legitimacy of that cause.
ERNEST BECKER,
Escape from Evil

The love of money is the root of evil.
1 Timothy

human beings like egg beaters, making waves. They are multitudinous and bodiless, made of color and sound. There is no hierarchy among them, not even a presiding Zeus. All of the gods have influence, but none has the power to rule absolutely. This is a list of the gods I know best:

God of Greed and Selfishness (always provoking, never listening)

God of Pain (inflicts sorrow mechanically, like Sisyphus pushing on his rock, without joy or regret)

Goddess of Healing (shadows Pain to nurse the wounded; dresses in pale green, the color of new shoots)

Goddess of Motherhood (two-faced: one warm, nurturing, caring; the other pinched and possessive)

God of Laughter (young and golden; Pan-like but found in apartments and delicatessens as well as sylvan glades; the genuine, pealing laughter of children)

Gods of Light, Beauty, the Arts (deep colors and clear, high voices)

God of Wisdom (an old, bearded, beautifully lined face; sees and evaluates to reflect truth without judgment)

Goddess of Mediation and Communication (neutral; tries to keep all doors open; probably pearl gray)

I'd like there to be a princely young Apollo or a powerful feminist Diana in my world, but I just don't see it that way. My gods are on an even keel, pushing and pulling to maneuver human beings into their particular power spheres. The lack of hierarchy means lots of commotion. I guess I experience it this way because I find life choices so difficult to make. Since I've always had a wide range of talent and potential, any new force that came along threatened to change my focus. When I was a little girl bandaging my dolls and dreaming of Florence Nightingale, the God of Healing had my allegiance. After that the God of Dance took hold, and later the God of Wisdom, but when my children were born I switched to the Great Maternal Goddess, trying to match her warm, open face. That's pretty much where I am now, raising a family and acting as general mediator between people.

Sometimes I imagine how different my life would be if I allowed a more passionate, less balanced pantheon of gods to exist. But right now, given my priorities, that isn't possible. Maybe in a dozen years when my kids are running on their own steam I'll be free to change the hierarchy and live more radically. For instance, I'd really like to elevate the God of Art above the God of Pain and settle down to the writing I've always wanted to do. It's not that I expect art to make milk and honey suddenly flow from trees, but I do believe that if people developed a greater capacity for experiencing each other there might be more music and light and laughter in the world. But I don't want you to think that I'm beating my wings against the bars of my cage. For now I'm content to let the deities go on stirring evenly around me.

—JANE is a wife and mother and an ardent journal keeper

FLYING IN AND OUT OF TIME

When you're high you are up and out, outside yourself, in the world. Elation means cutting loose from your self, connecting with what's out there.

When you're low you are down and in, withdrawn into yourself, away from the world. Depression means stuck on yourself, lost in thought, out of touch.

Consciousness as we usually experience it is separation. The I looks out at other I's and at the world and perceives that it is separate. I am *not* the chair, *not* the dog, *not* the other person. Separation is a neutral fact that may be experienced positively or negatively. Solitude is delicious; alienation is bitter. If one looks at the world through the barred windows of confinement it seems safer to remain in the prison of the self than to risk the strangeness beyond.

The strongest antidotes for alienated self-consciousness are love and hate. Meeting is merging. Loving and hating spring us free from isolation. An I can get lost in a tree, a stone, Bach's "Air for G String," the Brooklyn Bridge, or anything that attracts it.

The conditions for enjoying strange persons and strange things are identical: cease being a spectator and become a participant; disarm; decide to trust. Welcome what is alien and you will not be alone. When

This is an absolute necessity for anybody today. You must have a room, or a certain hour or so in a day, where you don't know what was in the newspapers that morning, you don't know who your friends are, you don't know what you owe anybody. . . . This is a place where you can simply experience and bring forth what you are and what you might be. This is the place of creative incubation. At first you may find that nothing happens there. But if you have a sacred place and use it, something eventually will happen.
JOSEPH CAMPBELL,
The Power of Myth

we give up our adversary stance, obsession with alienation eases up. We become freer; we lift off as lovers,
parts of some encompassing totality. In our highest
moments we are able to fly through time.

Breaking out of the isolation of the self is similar to
(perhaps identical with) the mystical union with the
divine life. Mystics of all ages have shared a vision of
the trustworthiness and unity of life. In this vision the
same divine life force animates people, cats, asparagus,
germs. Thus communion is a more ultimate fact than
alienation. Isolated self-consciousness is bad karma,
sin, illusion, or ignorance. All life is a part of the
cosmic dance. That's why getting high is a question of
transportation, of learning to travel from in to out,
from I to we, from self to world.

*In the orison of union,
the soul is fully awake
as regards God, but
wholly asleep as regards
things of this world. . . .
Thus does God, when
he raises a soul to union
with himself, suspend
the natural action of all
her faculties. She neither
sees, hears nor under-
stands, so long as she is
united with God. But
this time is always short
. . . God establishes
himself in the interior of
this soul in such a way,
that when she returns to
herself, it is wholly im-
possible for her to doubt
that she has been in
God, and God in her.*
SAINT TERESA

Viewpoints

Consciousness is always moving. On any day we may
travel from extreme isolation to ecstasy. In theory it's
easy to go from one extreme to the other: just turn
yourself inside out, make contact. In fact, it is tricky.
To travel freely in your interior space you need to
know how you keep yourself down and how you get
high. It may help to chart the daily and yearly
elevation changes in your consciousness.

- How, when, and where do you fly? Recall the times
  you and the world blended like lovers and there was
  no end to it. What boosts do you use to get high?
- How do you clip your wings, prevent yourself from
  soaring, depress yourself? Recall your most blue and
  desperate times. What tricks do you habitually use
  to heighten your paranoia and increase your isolation?
- Slip inside some ancient accounts of very high and
  very low states of consciousness, such as those found
  in the *Tibetan Book of the Dead,* the *Bhagavad Gita,* or
  Dante's *Divine Comedy,* and see how they fit you.

When Beethoven Sounds Like Toothpaste

No matter how much I like the way my life is, if I do the same things over and over sooner or later I start closing down, spinning in my own grooves. If you take a Beethoven sonata and play it fourteen hundred times, it eventually starts to sound like a toothpaste commercial! It's damn hard to live in stereophonic sound all the time. After a while I slip into a monotone; I start thinking the universe has stopped turning; that *my* thing is *the* thing, and it's a broken record.

Last December that was happening to me, so I took a light psychedelic one morning and walked down to the ocean. The beach was cold and gray and nearly deserted. Even though I had it all to myself I staked out a mile or so and set out to inspect my territory. At first I tried to worry about my life but I had been over my troubles so many times that I was bored with them, and anyway my body kept breaking out into movement. Soon I was running and leaping through the fog, cruising on automatic pilot, and anxiety didn't have a chance. I rolled up my pants and played in and out of the waves. A couple of dogs were chasing birds. I'd watched them do the same thing a thousand times before, but this time instead of a one-way pursuit I saw that they had a mutual tag game going! Birds and dogs picked worthy partners and played hilariously. I cheered for a certain bird; then a dog; then another bird; and they all played harder and harder, stimulated by the audience.

After several hours of moving and musing a clear, quiet voice inside my head said, *The universe is not hostile. Everything around you is all right.* Then I realized that *I* was all right too, exactly as I was, without qualification or future commitments or the benefit of someone else's generosity. There was nothing I had to do to qualify. (Qualify? For what? For whom?) The water and sand and fog and animals and I were perfectly compatible. I understood that my anxiety didn't have to do with my *existence,* but with the rules and values made up by human beings. A terrible pressure gave way in me as soon as I recalled that the human world isn't everything. . . .

—SID is a moody young psychic explorer

There is no hidden poet in me, just a little piece of God that might grow into poetry. And a camp needs a poet, one who experiences life there as a bard and is able to sing about it. At night, as I lay in the camp on my plank bed, surrounded by women and girls gently snoring, dreaming aloud, quietly sobbing . . . women and girls who often told me during the day, "We don't want to think . . . feel, otherwise we are sure to go out of our minds." I was sometimes filled with an infinite tenderness. . . .
And I prayed, "Let me be the thinking heart of these barracks." And that is what I want to be again. The thinking heart of a whole concentration camp.
ETTY HILLESUM,
An Interrupted Life

7

THE END AND THE BEGINNING

So long as human beings change and make history, so long as children are born and old people die, there will be tales to explain why sorrow darkens the day and stars fill the night. We invent stories about the origin and conclusion of life because we are exiles in the middle of time. The void surrounds us. We live within a parenthesis surrounded by question marks. Our stories and myths don't dispel ignorance, but they help us find our way, our place at the heart of the mystery. In the end, as in the beginning, there will be a vast silence, broken by the sound of one person telling a story to another.

Viewpoint

- Where did life come from? Where is it going? When will life, the world end? Make up a myth about the creation of the world. About its destiny.

The Joker Is Wild

Once there were two substances, water and earth, which had never touched. They floated timelessly in the darkness. There was neither time nor place nor process, but at the end of infinity water and earth bumped into each other. Water rolled against the land and stayed there, lapping the shore. This licking and tickling continued until one moment the edges of earth felt the motion and giggled. Consciousness was born, laughter was the child of this long relationship. Eventually the water's massage grew so intense that the land mass coughed bubbles of air under the sea, creating anima- tion. Sea creatures, popped from bubbles, crawled onto the land and grew into birds, kangaroos, centipedes, and hu- mans. The apes with the five-fingered hands found fire and claimed it, while explosions of birth and laughter swirled around them in musical spheres. Life multiplied, men and women named each other and made up stories, and death with her long hands took care of everything. But the human creatures who loved to make things fell into the habit of making each other, and soon there were so many feet on the land that laughter was stomped underground, crushed like summer grapes. So the people squeezed the carbonation from their bellies and strained upward, building theologies, skyscrapers, arguments, missiles. Soon they stood heart to heart, pushing and jumping to make room for their own, so that laughter was forced to the very center of the earth. The land bore it until she could hold no longer. Then her great axial bones cracked like glass and bombs of laughter shot forth, opening up the earth. All creatures were swallowed together. Again there was stillness, only water lapping against the land.

*We shall not cease from exploration
And the end of all our exploring
Will be to arrive where we started
And know the place for the first time
When the last of earth left to discover
Is that which was the beginning
At the source of the longest river
The voice of the hidden waterfall.*
T. S. Eliot,
Four Quartets

—ANYONE ANYWHERE, EVERYONE EVERYWHERE